Advance Praise for
What All Children Want Their Parents to Know

"Finally — a parenting book filled with great ideas from a child's perspective! This exceptional book will empower parents to raise happy, unstoppable children into even more of their greatness!"

— Cynthia Kersey, author of *Unstoppable* and
Unstoppable Women

"Parents will want to keep this book close at hand — it's so much more than a one-time read! This is the kind of parenting book you'll refer to time and time again. It's a simple yet profound guide to positive parenting."

— Holly Bea, author of *God Believes in You* and
Good Night God

"Diana Loomans 'gets it' more than anyone else I know. How wonderful that she and her daughter have created these pearls of wisdom for families everywhere. Parents will greatly benefit from this book, no matter what the age of their children. Study it and live it!"

—Lissa Coffey, author of *What's Your Dosha, Baby?:*
Discover the Vedic Way for Compatibility in Life and Love

"Decade upon decade, we parents have been told to 'listen to the experts' so our children will grow up happy and whole. What a breath of fresh air to find authors who believe we must listen to the children themselves! In *What All Children Want Their Parents to Know,* Diana and Julia give practical advice on how to pick up on the way children express needs and react to the behavior of others, including ours! Page after page, stories abound — some humorous, some gripping, some heartrending, and all vehicles for an important message: unconditional love, the most powerful and empowering force in the universe, is the essential ingredient to happiness for all adults, children, and families."

—Elisa Medhus, MD, author of *Raising Children Who Think for Themselves* and *Hearing is Believing*

"This book is a superb how-to manual for the most important profession in the world! It offers parents the needed skills to transform the spirit inside of every child, and propel tomorrow's leaders into their full potential!"

—B. J. Dohrmann, president of The International Learning Trust and host of *American Dreamer*

What All Children Want
Their Parents to Know

12 Keys to Raising
a Happy Child

DIANA LOOMANS
with Julia Godoy

An H J Kramer Book

published in a joint venture with

New World Library

An H J Kramer Book
published in a joint venture with
New World Library

Editorial office: Administrative office:
P.O. Box 1082   14 Pamaron Way
Tiburon, California 94920   Novato, California 94949

Text design and typography by Tona Pearce Myers

Library of Congress Cataloging-in-Publication Data
Loomans, Diana.
  What all children want their parents to know : 12 keys to raising a happy child / Diana Loomans with Julia Godoy.
      p.   cm.
Includes index.
ISBN 1-932073-13-2 (pbk. : alk. paper)
1. Parenting. 2. Child rearing. 3. Parent and child. I. Godoy, Julia, 1977– II. Title.
HQ755.8.L666 2005
306.874—dc22   2004029815

First printing, May 2005
ISBN 1-932073-13-2
ISBN 13 978-1-932073-13-3
Printed in Canada on partially recycled, acid-free paper
Distributed to the trade by Publishers Group West

10 9 8 7 6 5 4 3 2 1

*This book is dedicated
to every precious child living on this earth,
and to the devoted parents who love them.*

CONTENTS

by Dr. Bernie Siegel

I found this book to be full of wisdom and an excellent resource for perplexed parents who care. As the father of five I can attest to the effectiveness of the methods outlined herein.

Parenting is the world's number one health issue. As a physician who counsels people with life-threatening illnesses, I have learned that those who grow up loved are a minority. I also know that if every child grew up loved by parents who had read this book and practiced its wisdom, the world would not be experiencing wars. The unloved are seeking, through their various addictions, the feelings of love and belonging they never received from their parents. They have grown up with beliefs to die by and not beliefs to live by.

If parents treated their children as well as they do their pets we would have healthier, happier children. When in doubt ask yourself, what would a loving grandparent do? It is not an accident that we have children and our children have our grandchildren and their children have our great grand-children. The difference is in the maturity and ability to love unconditionally that comes to us with time.

Parents provide their children with both physical and psychological genes. *What All Children Want Their Parents to Know* will help you provide your children with the highest quality psychological genes and enable them to live long, healthy lives. It is time to leave behind your personal family experience and tragedy. My hope is that every parent reads this book and learns from its easily understood practical wisdom.

I learned a great deal from our children. When I lost my temper our son, who is a lawyer today, would say, "Go ahead and hit me. It will hurt you more than it does me." But the son who ended any thought I had of ever spanking a child again said, "If you hit me, I'll call the police. I am a person."

Helen Keller said that deafness is darker by far than blindness. So listen to your children and heal your family. When a child grows up with self-love and self-acceptance her parents have produced a happy child and a happy child is a success.

What do children really want their parents to know, and what do children need to grow into thriving adults? If kids could speak from the depths of their hearts, what would they want to say to their parents — the people who will influence them more than anyone else?

This book addresses these vital questions — from a child's perspective. It offers twelve powerful keys to raising a happy, responsible, and fulfilled child, based on the popular poem "What All Children Want Their Parents to Know." My daughter and I wrote the poem to represent the collective voice of children and to express the desires they most want the significant adults in their lives to know.

Each chapter is devoted to one of the stanzas and is filled with hands-on stories and ideas designed with the busy family in mind, including several exercises at the end of each chapter. Since most parents have a deep desire to give their children the very best, and kids don't come with instruction manuals, this book offers practical guidelines to providing children with what they most need — one step at a time. Read through each chapter, do the suggested exercises, and post the poem, printed in its entirety on the following pages, in a place where you'll see it every day.

By taking the time to read this book, you'll focus on what's really important and create more special moments. Many of a child's most treasured memories of childhood happen in these small, magnificent moments.

WHAT ALL CHILDREN WANT
THEIR PARENTS TO KNOW

Teach me to love and care for myself
Through your own positive example.
I'll learn from all your actions
And grow to have good self-care.

Notice me often,
Taking joy in my very existence.
I'll grow up knowing I'm special
And help others to feel the same.

Listen to me with empathy,
Have an open and loving heart.
I'll know I'm seen and heard
And grow to be a good listener.

Laugh and have fun with me often,
Be affectionate every day.
I'll play and enjoy my life
And bring more joy to others.

Acknowledge me often,
And tell me when you appreciate me.
I'll know that I am worthy
And learn to acknowledge others.

Teach me to be disciplined,
And correct me with kindness.
I'll lead a life of dignity,
With the pride of self-respect.

Allow room for me to grow,
To make mistakes and have opinions.
I'll learn to be independent
And to trust my own judgment.

Stay interested in learning
And following your dreams.
I'll pick up your enthusiasm
And be inspired to do the same.

Be honest and authentic,
And live your highest values.
I'll learn from your experiences
And grow to have integrity.

Teach me to be of service
And to honor the differences in others.
I'll learn generosity of spirit
And embrace all walks of life.

Focus on what's going right
And have faith during troubled times.
I'll learn the skill of optimism,
With gratitude for each new day.

Love me without condition,
Throughout my ups and downs.
I'll know that I am cherished
And bring more love to the world.

— DIANA LOOMANS AND JULIA GODOY

CHAPTER ONE

Teach by Example

Teach me to love and care for myself
Through your own positive example.
I will learn from all your actions
And grow to have good self-care.

One of the deepest desires in every parent's heart is to raise a healthy and happy child whose life is meaningful and fulfilling. Most parents spare no expense to make this possible, working hard to provide a nice home, proper health care, good schools, fun toys, and extracurricular activities. All these things contribute to a child's quality of life and well-being, but they cannot fulfill the deep longing that resides in every child, which is to see their parents taking good care of themselves and experiencing their own joy and happiness.

Kids seem to instinctively know that a happy, well-adjusted adult has much more joy, attention, energy, and love to impart than an adult who is stressed, overworked, or overextended. The image of using an oxygen mask on an airplane is fitting — only the adult who takes in enough oxygen first can be helpful to the young who are dependent on him or her for life support.

Put Your Own Self-Care First

Above all things, revere yourself.

— PYTHAGORAS

The first and most pivotal way to be a role model for children of all ages lies in the healthy, consistent care of *you*. Parents sometimes fall into the habit of putting all their children's needs before their own, under the pretense that children always come first. Clearly there are times when this is this case, as when a baby has croup in the middle of the night; then it is appropriate to place all the attention on the baby's wellness. And when a special event such as a birthday, graduation, or performance comes up, everyone naturally focuses on the special child for the day. But under normal circumstances, it is practical for parents to pay quality attention to their own lives first, knowing that a small amount of daily self-care is *oxygen for the spirit*. This translates into a calmer adult who reacts less often and responds with more perspective and grace.

When I was in grade school, my mother, who had four children, was advised by her doctor to take up swimming for health reasons. At first she was overwhelmed and wondered where she'd find the time to fit this into her schedule. To complicate matters further, my parents didn't have a second car, and there was no gymnasium within walking distance.

But with a little ingenuity and a lot of determination, my

mother came up with a plan that would support her health and model the idea of putting her self-care first. She paid a visit to the nearby high school and struck up a conversation with the girls' gym coach. Before leaving, she boldly asked the coach if she would be willing to admit her into the freshman's beginning swim class. Not quite knowing what to make of my mother, the coach said she'd check with school authorities and get back to her. Within days, my jubilant mom was admitted to class, making her the oldest freshman student ever to attend a beginners' swim class!

Swimming did not come easily to her, since she had never learned to swim as a child. I remember seeing my mom practicing and sputtering in the bathroom sink as she struggled to get the rhythm of the crawl down, dipping her face in and out of the water and sometimes choking as she attempted to master this new challenge. I will never forget the day she came home from her first day of successfully doing the crawl in the Olympic-size pool. She was filled with a sense of accomplishment I hadn't seen in her for a long time.

Her commitment to her self-care kept her swimming at the high school pool for a number of years. She became such a good swimmer that she began to tutor the "scaredy-cats like me," as she put it. Even though it meant that she was not there on certain days when we arrived home from school, it was always a plus, since she returned refreshed and invigorated.

My daughter, Julia, has fond memories of walking with "Granny" to the high school pool and swimming alongside her as they pretended to be mermaids together. Julia attributes her lifelong passion for swimming to those early days when her grandmother made it into such a fun adventure. What a wonderful effect my mother's simple act of self-care has had on the entire family over the years.

A small amount of self-care can bring an extraordinary amount of balance and serenity to you as a parent and to the whole family. For some, self-care takes the form of daily meditation; for others, a brisk walk or an early morning workout sets the tone for the day. Many adults find that by taking five minutes or less to plan the day, they save much time in the long run.

The key question to ask yourself is, What do I need as a daily dose of positive energy? Even if you can muster up just five minutes to set your intentions for the day or to do a few yoga poses, the return is worth its weight in gold.

Do What You Say and Say What You Do

What you are shouts so loudly in my ears,
I can't hear what you say.

— RALPH WALDO EMERSON

Words without action have little or no impact. But when words are backed by living examples, they have the power to form beliefs and habits that can last a lifetime. Mahatma Gandhi understood the value of practicing what he preached and stopped at nothing to be a living example of what he taught. A distressed mother once visited Gandhi with her young child, greeting him with a single request: "Mahatma, please tell my child to stop eating so much sugar!"

"Bring her back in three days," was all that Gandhi said. Bewildered, the woman and her child departed and returned in exactly three days. When Gandhi saw them again, he looked into the child's eyes and simply said, "Stop eating sugar," to her surprise.

"Forgive me, Mahatma, but couldn't you have told my daughter this three days ago?" the woman inquired. "No, madam. Three days ago, I hadn't stopped eating sugar yet," Mahatma said with a grin. As unnecessary as this gesture may have seemed to the woman, Gandhi understood the importance of speaking from firsthand experience to have a lasting impact.

The power of influence by example works in reverse as well. Children who grow up in family systems ravaged by violence, alcoholism, depression, obesity, drug addiction, anger, verbal abuse, criticism, favoritism, or neglect have a much greater chance of contending with these same problems as they grow up. How can a child hope not to have a weight problem when living with a compulsive overeater? How many teens can bypass substance abuse when an addicted parent or family member in the household is not seeking help? How many adults never even entertain what their dreams or potential might be, suffering from low self-esteem after years of criticism and put-downs?

Saying, "Do what I say, not what I do" rarely has an effect. A child almost always acts on what is demonstrated rather than on what is said. Poor modeling, unfortunately, has a powerful impact on children, even when they witness the devastating consequences. It is a known fact that over 75 percent of all prison inmates have had one or more family members who were in jail. The following story serves as a good example of this dynamic. Steven, a thirty-three-year-old man and long-time friend of mine, spent his last twelve years serving a sentence for armed robbery. He ran away from home at fifteen and had been robbing gas stations and neighborhood convenience stores for over five years before he was finally caught.

"It was almost a relief when I was caught," he said, "because I knew it was just a matter of time. My father and a few of my uncles all served time. I guess I got set up for a life of crime more than I'd realized."

Fortunately for him, his father, having served a similar sentence, came to his aid while his son was serving his sentence. "It was a turning point in my life the first time my dad showed up to see me in prison," he said. "I hadn't seen him since my thirteenth birthday. He was serving time before I ran away."

Before the young man could speak, his father blurted out, "Son, I'm not here to blame you — if anyone is to blame, it's me for not being a good father. I'm here to help you now. It's time we break this cycle for good." They shared a moment when all the barriers dropped away, and for the first time the young man saw a tear run down his father's cheek. Twice a month from then on, until his sentence was over, his father came to see him. With his dad's support, he got his GED and an associate degree in computer science while serving time.

There is no question that an adult's choices and actions can have lifelong effects on his or her children. In the areas where we are strong, we build strength in our children and the world. In the areas where we are weak, it is never too late to turn the tide.

Follow Your Heart

Go confidently in the direction of your dreams.
Live the life you've imagined.

— HENRY DAVID THOREAU

Far too many adults have put a stranglehold on their hearts' desires by neglecting the things they most wish to do in favor of tasks they've decided they *should* do. As a life coach, I have witnessed the many ways that adults *should* on themselves: "I want to take dance classes, but I *should* spend more time with the kids." Why not take them along? "I'd love to work in radio, but I *should* stick with my reliable but boring day job." How about making the transition slowly? "I'd love to live in a place with a view, but I *should* stick with my cozy little home that is paid for." Why not get the financial advice needed to make the move at an opportune time? "I'd love to go on a vacation, but I *should* use the money to make a responsible investment." How about doing both, even if it takes a little longer? Over time, our runaway shoulds imprison us in a dull lifestyle that neither excites nor ignites us.

What does that model for our children? A life full of *shoulds* sends the message that we can't have what we really want…that we aren't worth it…that dreams are for other people…that settling is okay. A number of years ago on a weekend adventure in Arizona, I sat before a large bonfire with a group of friends at the end of a long, adventurous day. Since I like to ask thought-provoking questions, I asked the group, "If time, money, and responsibility were no object, what would you be doing with your life right now, and why?"

The answers that spewed forth, from the kids as well as the adults, were fascinating and riveting. One of the women — a thirty-something single mother sitting beside her eleven-year-old son — sat very quietly as the others spoke, staring into the fire with a forlorn look on her face. Finally, I asked her if she would be willing to share what was in her heart. "I am thinking about how impossible my wish is," she said with a sigh. "How can you be so sure?" I challenged her. "Yeah, Mom," her son added, "tell us what it is, and we'll decide how impossible it is!"

With a little more persuasion, she agreed to share what

she would be doing if there were no obstacles in her way. It turns out that instead of running her small home-cleaning service, which she disliked intensely, she'd move to Wyoming and start a horseback riding school, which would suit her interests in teaching, horses, and living in the country.

Before long we were all enlisted, offering ideas to help her see that her idea was not just a pipe dream but a real possibility if she created a game plan and followed it. Five years later, she is thriving in Wyoming, teaching riding lessons at a ranch, with a few horses of her own. Her son is thriving as well, working as a ranch hand for some of the locals.

A simple fireside conversation five years ago changed the course of this woman's life. Once she dared to dream, and to express that dream to a circle of supportive friends, she became unstoppable. Her son has watched her transform from a downtrodden woman in a rut to an energized, uplifted woman following her dream. One can only wonder what aspirations he may have for himself as a result of her invigorating influence.

Take a Role Model Inventory

Live so that you wouldn't be ashamed to sell
the family parrot to the town gossip.

— WILL ROGERS

How many of us stop to consider the effect we are having on our children with the thoughts we think and the lifestyles we have? Albert Schweitzer was so convinced that being an example was the superior way to teach that he once said, "Setting an example is the only real teaching there is."

In a retreat weekend I have led for families, one of the most powerful exercises is called "Role Model Inventory." It came about when a brave father asked his adult son, "Tell me, what is the best thing that I have taught you over the years through example, and what is the worst thing that I have modeled for you through my actions? How have each affected you?" His son, while caught off guard by the candor of the question, answered with little hesitation.

"Well Dad, the best thing that you have modeled for me is your fresh and wise perspective on just about everything. Every time I have ever come to you with a problem or concern, you have helped me to find the best solution.

"You also bring a great perspective to many things that others would find mundane or overwhelming. I can't even name how many times your influence has helped me to make the right decision for myself. I am a much more hopeful, resourceful, and creative person because of it!"

He reflected for a moment and then went on to say, "The worst thing that you have taught me through your actions is your drive to always want to be at the next level — somewhere other than where you are. It leaves you with a certain sort of dissatisfaction, and you often seem restless.

"I've struggled a lot to find peace and satisfaction because I'm often second-guessing whether it's okay for me to be where I am. There's nothing I'd like more, Dad, than to see you content and happy with your life the way it is! There will always be the next level, and it saddens me to see you missing out on so much."

This man took a big risk in asking his son such a brave question, and his son was courageous in giving him a straight answer. They both felt that it was one of the best talks they'd ever had. This fifty-something father is diligently practicing being more present and appreciating his life here and now, knowing that it is *more than enough the way it is.*

The following exercises will help you to practice some of the most important ideas covered in this chapter.

Exercises

1. Self-Care Check-In

Ask yourself these questions: What best serves me as my *daily self-care routine,* to be practiced whether I have five minutes or fifty minutes to devote to it? (For example, planning the day, praying, reading, journaling, meditating, reviewing your goals, visualizing, stretching, or exercising).

What do I consider to be *supreme self-care,* when I have the luxury of extra time? How often will I make time for this? (For example, a massage, a weekend retreat or spa getaway, an afternoon hike, Sunday brunch).

2. Role Model Inventory

Write down the best thing that each of your parents taught you through their positive example, and the worst thing that each of them modeled through example. Ask your child what the best thing is that you have taught them through your own good example (if you have more than one child, the answers may vary), and what the worst thing is that you have role modeled thus far.

If your children are too young to answer, ask a significant family member or friend for honest feedback. This exercise offers an inside look at the way you appear to your child and a chance to take what works and to transform the rest while there's still time!

A MESSAGE FROM ALL CHILDREN ABOUT
TEACHING BY EXAMPLE

Dear Parent or Guardian,
The way you live your life
Will be my greatest influence.

When you neglect your own needs,
You teach me low self-esteem.
When you care for your well-being,
You teach me about self-love.

When you break your word,
You teach me inconsistency.
When you act on your word,
You teach me to follow through.

So please take good care of yourself
And be a role model in my life.
When you live what you teach,
I will grow up to do the same.

CHAPTER TWO

Spend Quality Time Daily

Notice me often,
Taking joy in my very existence.
I'll grow up knowing I'm special
And help others to feel the same.

The Talmud says, "Every blade of grass has its Angel that bends over it and whispers, 'Grow, grow.'" One of the most significant contributions one can make in the world is to be that angel for a special child. Find joy in their existence, encourage their every step, and share quality moments with them often. Quality time can be defined as taking time to revel in your child, without any preoccupations or distractions. To revel is to take intense satisfaction in the existence of another — to feel one's heart swell with cherishing.

At a parenting workshop I facilitated, a participant shared some touching memories of a beloved great-uncle

from her childhood who made her feel like the most important child in the world each time they were together. She
considered her Uncle Clyde a "revel-master" and affectionately described him as follows:

> He was an amazing person who was fifty-something-going-
> on-five. He was forever young at heart and took pleasure in
> the small things more than anyone I'd ever known. He loved
> to surprise me in the simplest and kindest of ways, often
> bringing gifts from nature. One day when he came to visit,
> he carefully brought a branch out from behind his back. To
> my surprise, perched on the stick was a large green caterpil-
> lar edging its way along the knobby branch. "This caterpil-
> lar is a living miracle," he told me. "Before long, she'll be
> fluttering through the skies as a beautiful butterfly!"
>
> He gave me the stick and gazed at me intently, until I
> finally asked him what he was doing. "I'm watching you
> while there's still time, before you transform into a beau-
> tiful butterfly!" I blushed and said nothing, but I took in
> what he said more than he may have known.
>
> Whenever I would talk to him or tell him a story, he
> would tilt his head in wonder, sigh, and widen his already
> large round eyes. Sometimes it made me stop and laugh out
> loud. In his presence, I would talk a little bit louder and
> express myself with more conviction and confidence, almost
> singing with exuberance to have such an avid listening audi-
> ence! Sometimes I would rehearse stories I wanted to tell
> him, anticipating the way he would clap his hands together
> and laugh his hearty laugh. I couldn't wait to be near him.
>
> The very best thing about Uncle Clyde was his ability
> to revel in a way that made me feel as though I was the
> most remarkable miracle he'd ever laid eyes on. Every move
> I made seemed magical in his presence. With him, I knew
> beyond any doubt that I had to be the most fascinating kid

in the whole wide world! To be seen as an ultimate treasure is an experience that I wish for every child on earth. If everyone received this kind of attention, the world would be full of happy, confident human beings.

My Uncle Clyde passed away when I turned twenty-one. Shortly before he died, he made me promise to make the funeral a celebration. He quietly reminded me, "I'm not really dying. I'm just graduating from life!" True to my word, I released a bundle of colorful balloons at the close of the service, along with one large, beautiful monarch butterfly. And I just knew that Uncle Clyde was somewhere out there, taking a big sigh and gazing at all of us with wonder.

When she had finished her inspiring description of her uncle, I asked the room of more than one hundred participants how many of them had ever been cherished in quite this way. Ten people raised their hands. When I asked how many of these fortunate few had experienced this from a parent, five hands went up.

My next question was, How many of you have experienced this from both parents? Only one person raised his hand. People's surprised responses could be heard throughout the room. We were all silent for an instant, struck by how rare it is to be reveled in. In a room of more than one hundred people, only one had experienced the priceless gift of being thoroughly loved by both parents.

What an unspeakable joy it is for a child to have one or more significant adults love them this way. And what a dreadful loss it is for children who have never known the delight of this kind of soul sustenance. We can do no greater good than to help children know how special they are. Children with healthy self-esteem will grow up to revel in others, in turn helping them feel special and whole.

Quantity Is Silver; Quality Is Gold

The little things... the little moments... they aren't little.

— JON KABAT-ZINN

Quality time is not a substitute for quantity of time, but most children would rather have an hour of sheer fun and attention from a significant adult than a much bigger block of more predictable or mundane time.

Arthur, a relative of ours, is an overworked father who realized the value of spending quality time with his twin sons after he divorced their mother. He was as busy as he had ever been, launching a new company and often working up to eighty hours a week. He had recently relocated and remarried, with a new wife and a newborn baby. He was under mounting pressures, yet his twelve-year-old twin sons were still precious to him.

Amid the bustle and chaos of his life, Arthur seemed to be completely consumed. Months began to roll by without much contact with his boys. While they knew that their dad loved them, it was difficult for them to understand why he was no longer available to them. They adored their father, and although they tried to accept the explanations for his absence, they had their own emotions of abandonment and loss to contend with. They felt neglected and began to fear that their father didn't love them as much as he loved his new job and family.

Their grades began to decline, and their behavior at school started to deteriorate. An attentive school counselor offered suggestions to the frazzled, overworked father, who was wearing thin from all the demands. The boys' lives were troubled because of his absence, and he knew that something must be done. The counselor reminded him of the powerful influence that his presence had on their lives, and that even a few hours of quality time a month could be invaluable. The father proceeded to block out a day in his calendar once a month that he left wide open to go on outings with his sons. He let them know they could choose whatever they most wanted to do with him.

Most of their choices involved little, if any, cost. Going to the park to play basketball or catch, riding bikes, hiking, wrestling, playing with the dog, watching movies, or playing video games together seemed to be at the top of their list. During his time with them, he made a point to ask his sons about their friends, activities, and lives at home and school.

The twin boys, now doing well in high school, said they have had more memorable times in those twelve days out of the year than they remembered having when their father lived with them. With more than 50 percent of all American families living in divided households, the art of creating quality moments has never been more significant. Sharing even twelve quality days a year will have a long-lasting impact on a child, making all the difference.

Transform Quantity Time into Quality Time

Nothing is as important as this day.

— JOHANN WOLFGANG VON GOETHE

Recent studies show that most parents spend about thirty minutes a week of quality time with each child. This comes out to two hours a month, and twenty-four hours a year. With 8,760 hours in a single year, twenty-four hours a year comes to one-quarter of 1 percent of the total hours in a year. Is that really enough?

When we tally up the number of hours most parents spend providing for a child in a week — laundering; shopping for food and clothing; preparing meals; cleaning up; driving to school, appointments, and activities; and overseeing homework and household tasks — it is easy to see that many hours are spent each week just performing needed tasks. Every parent deserves accolades for this munificent offering of time and energy week after week.

Since these perfunctory tasks will never go away, the key is to transform more of them into memorable moments. Quantity time becomes quality time when you include anything that is of interest to your child. A three-year-old will delight in helping to fold laundry if you incorporate every three-year-old's favorite pastime, which is playing make-believe! An eight-year-old will happily go food shopping with you and help hunt for food in the various aisles, especially if you let her select a special treat for being so helpful.

Beginning in early grade school, if not before, kids love to listen to music. Why not occasionally play their CDs while driving together as a way to stay connected to their music and their world? When there is garage cleanup or outdoor yard work to do, playing catch on breaks can be a great way to add laughter and play to a parent and child's day. Most teens will gladly go on errands with you if you incorporate a driving lesson or stop at their favorite store on the way home. Let your child's interests be your guide in bringing more quality moments into your time together. What children of all ages most want is to be noticed, heard, seen, understood, and interacted with.

Create More Memorable Moments

Forever is composed of a series of nows.

— EMILY DICKINSON

My mother, Diana, has a way of creating out-of-the-ordinary golden moments, and she has done so for as long as I can remember. Even though I am now an adult, I still value the surprising moments that she creates out of the blue as much as I did when I was a child.

Just last week, my mom and I were in the middle of a short phone conversation when suddenly she interrupted with, "Julia, I just have to tell you something before it slips through the moment. Yesterday, when I was with you and Anthony [my husband], I was so happy just being around both of you — there are so many great things in your lives right now — your love for each other, the baby on the way, your new place, and exciting new work projects for both of you. I just wanted you to know how inspiring it is to be around both of you while you are in such a privileged and enriching time of life."

I was really caught off guard. I'd spent the morning doing heaps of laundry and lamenting over the laborious unpacking process that was part of our recent move. I was feeling overwhelmed by how many hours my husband was working that week, and my lower back was in pain related to the move and the pregnancy. On top of that, I was behind in my hours on a work project and in need of some extra sleep more than anything else.

"Thanks," was all I could say at the moment. Later that day, and for the rest of the week, I took in her words as I went about the tasks on the extra long to-do list before me. The idea that everything going on was a privilege had a time-release effect on me. It energized me and helped me to realize that my life was wonderful here and now. I wanted to take it all in, and not wait until the house was in order, the laundry done, and the work project complete before I could be at peace. It took my mom sixty seconds to say what she did, but the impact that her words had on me stayed with me for days, perhaps even longer.

Now Is All There Is

What is essential is invisible to the eye.
Only with the heart can one see rightly.

— ANTOINE DE SAINT-EXUPÉRY

A few years ago, a good friend experienced the death of his teen daughter and only child, who died in a tragic accident while away at summer camp. He was stricken with grief for many months and suffered from what he called an "all-pervasive regret" that, to this day, he still grapples with.

His regret is all too common — that of not having spent enough quality time with Sara, his beloved daughter. Being a busy businessman who frequently traveled, and going through a divorce when his daughter was eleven, didn't lend itself to day-to-day in-person contact, and as Sara matured, he found that days of not seeing her sometimes turned into weeks. Although he felt they had good rapport, and though they stayed in touch by phone, he now realizes how much more he could have involved himself in her life. "If I'd known that we'd have just sixteen short years together, things would have been much different. I'd have worked less and done so much more with her. I would have talked more about important things, taken her more places, and told her how I felt about her much more often."

Listening to him reminded me that now is all that any of us ever has. The only moment that we can ever be sure of is the present one. The past is over, and the future hasn't happened yet. I wrote the following poem in memory of Sara and in honor of my dear friend. It has been reprinted in many newsletters and publications, and I hope that it reminds families of all walks of life that now is the time to say what needs to be said. Now is the best opportunity to appreciate and enjoy the good fortune of love, family, and the joy of spending time together.

REMEMBER

Remember when you were two
and you scribbled all over my college paper?
I thought you'd cry when I yelled at you.
But you didn't.

Remember when you were six
and I missed your school play working late?
I thought you'd resent me.
But you didn't.

Remember when you were eleven
and I told you that your mom and I
loved you very much,
but that we would no longer be living together?
I thought you'd drift from me.
But you didn't.

There were lots of things you didn't do.
You didn't stop giving me big bear hugs.
You didn't close your heart after I moved out.
You didn't stop making me those wonderful
homemade birthday cards.
And you didn't ever stop loving me.

And there were so many things
I wanted to make up to you
and do for you
when you returned from camp
your sixteenth summer.
But you didn't.

Exercises

1. Book Quality Time Now

Mark your calendar for the next twelve months with a special day to be set aside once a month for spending with your child. Make these blocks of time as important as a business or doctor's appointment — not to be changed unless there is an emergency, so that your child knows how important this *special time* really is.

2. Practice Becoming a "Revel-master"

Just for today, take the time to revel in a child and to give your undivided attention and appreciation, even if only for sixty seconds.

3. Turn Quantity Time into Quality Time

Since we all spend so many hours each week doing perfunctory tasks and everyday jobs, find as many ways as possible to make these moments fun and meaningful. Sing songs, give hugs, share laughter, act out characters, tell stories, have discussions, dance, play word games and guessing games, listen to music or tapes, and make the mundane memorable and even magnificent.

~

A MESSAGE FROM ALL CHILDREN ABOUT
QUALITY TIME AND ATTENTION

Dear Parent or Guardian,
The time and attention you give me
Will greatly affect my self-worth.

When you neglect to give me your time,
You teach me to feel insignificant.
When you give me your quality time,
You teach me that I am important.

When your attention is divided,
You teach me to feel unnoticed.
When you show me undivided interest,
You teach me that I am valued.

So please take the time to notice me,
Take in what I do and say.
I'll grow up knowing I'm exceptional
And be more attentive to others.

CHAPTER THREE

Practice True Listening

Listen to me with empathy,
Have an open and loving heart.
I'll know I'm seen and heard
And grow to be a good listener.

To be a good listener is an admirable quality that assures us of having a host of supportive friends and a community for a lifetime. A person who knows how to listen gives the priceless gifts of their presence and care. After being in the company of a good listener, we have a feeling of satisfaction and fullness — even if the topic of conversation has been difficult.

True Listening Is Rare

We would have two ears and one tongue
so that we would listen more and talk less.

— DIOGENES

Most of us have rarely been truly listened to, and we savor the occasion when it happens. Observe any dialogue, and you'll notice that most people quickly steer a conversation back to themselves or their own interests. When a person says, "I'm not feeling well," the average response might be, "I had a touch of the flu last week myself, and I didn't feel well for three days." A good listener might respond with, "Tell me more" or, "Really? When did you begin to feel this way?" or, "I'm sorry to hear that. Is there any way I can help?" A good listener stays with the one talking and finds out more.

Young children are keenly aware when an adult is truly listening to them, since it is not an everyday occurrence for most kids. A woman by the name of Laura, director of a local day care center, possesses the charismatic quality of being a true listener. She is so present to the children that she seems to listen with every ounce of her, and the kids all love her! She strokes each child's hair, holds their hands, touches their faces, or picks them up as they talk to her. Children gravitate to her, and they climb all over her five-foot-ten frame as though she were a great oak tree! They love to tell her all manner of interesting tidbits, from new sibling arrivals to the bubblegum that got stuck in their hair the night before.

Laura responds to each story with animation, inviting the children with her dramatic expressions to tell her more. "You have a brand-new baby sister? I'll bet she sleeps a whole lot," she might say while pretending to charily hold a sleeping infant. "You got orange bubblegum in your hair last night?" she might ask. "Oh, my, we better find my great big Jolly Green Giant scissors!"

The children never have any trouble coming up with stories to tell her, both real and fabricated, and they flock around her every chance they can, waiting to share their latest captivating adventures.

Overcome the "Half-Listening Syndrome"

True listening is love in action.

— M. SCOTT PECK

Because true listening is rare, people often listen to one another without really hearing what has been said. Adults may become so lost in thought that they begin to suffer from the dreaded *HLS* (half-listening syndrome), which leaves room for being only partially present at best. Every child over the age of one recognizes the symptoms of *HLS* — the tense, distracted, or faraway expressions and the rote responses to whatever is being said, such as "mmhmm," "not right now," or "can't you see Mommy's busy?"

The frustration that mounts when a child realizes there is no way to rouse an adult from half-listening is palpable and frequently results in the child becoming ornery or acting out in some disagreeable way to get the needed attention. When my daughter, Julia, was very young, she developed a strategy to bring me, quite literally, to my knees whenever I was not really listening to her. She would determinedly tug on my legs until I would finally crouch down to her eye level. Then she would cup her little hands on either side of my face and say, "Now I can see you, Mommy." What she really meant was *now I could see her* — and like all children, she yearned to be seen as well as heard.

A young man in his mid-forties experienced the passing of his mother with a great sorrow that took him by surprise since they were not close and she had been ill for a number of years before she died. Ben had a difficult time getting to the bottom of what seemed like an endless well of grief. "What I finally realized was that in all my forty-six years, I didn't feel that my mother ever really listened to me. She talked *at* me rather than *with* me, and because she was chronically depressed, she often looked *past* me, rather than *at* me when she was talking to me."

He can hardly remember a time when his mother was truly present. What was most distressing to him was the realization that he would never in this lifetime experience the often dreamed-of conversations with his mother in which she would find his ideas interesting, laugh at his jokes, or be compelled by his presence. He had to face the fact that his mother was gone, and that she hadn't seen or known him the way he'd wished for. Sadly, he felt that he never really knew her either. On the evening of her funeral, he was awake all night, crying in the arms of his wife saying over and over, "I never knew her...and she never knew me."

While it seemed an irreconcilable loss for him, over time it filled him with a new sense of conviction — to reveal himself more to the people he most cared about and to listen better to everyone he came in contact with, in honor of the mother he dearly loved but never really knew.

Four Steps to True Listening

A good listener is a rarity to be treasured.

— THE DALAI LAMA

Imagine how much more prepared we would be for life if we'd taken a course entitled "Listening 101" by the time we were ten, followed by another course entitled "Advanced Listening Skills" by the time we left the sixth grade!

Most of us only half-learn the skill of listening. If we are superbly fortunate, we learn from someone who imparts this skill by modeling it him- or herself. Children who can listen intently to others are few and far between. And kids who are skilled at listening to a peer's side of a conflict without having a knee-jerk reaction are an even rarer breed.

Countless children have never been taught the vital skill of listening well when given instructions or directions. Imagine the host of human challenges large and small that could be prevented by the simple act of listening without distraction or defense. I designed the following four-part formula to help people of all ages develop the vital skill of true listening. It can be used at home, in the classroom, or in any group, including business settings:

Step One: Listen fully. Focus completely on the person speaking. Hold direct eye contact, show care and interest, and hear what is being said with an open mind and heart. Most important, listen without judgment of any kind. This helps create a safe atmosphere, which encourages engaging conversation.

Step Two: Listen without giving feedback. The second step of true listening is usually the most challenging. Remain quiet as another speaks, despite what thoughts, perceptions, or opinions may surface. This will spur the speaker on to reveal more and to move into a deeper dialogue. Save comments or suggestions for later, and only if asked. If you say anything at all, use words that will bring out the speaker even more, such as, "Tell me more" or, "What happened next?"

Step Three: Repeat what is being said. The most frequent error that most listeners make at this point is attempting to solve the problem at hand or to share their own thoughts or experiences, rather than staying with the one talking. Instead, repeat back what is being said to show that you are really getting it: "So, it sounds like you're really irritated about this" or, "You seem very happy about that." The simple act of mirroring helps a person to feel heard and to understand more of his or her own feelings and needs.

Step Four: Ask questions rather than giving opinions. At some point, the person talking will most likely want feedback from you. The most valuable response that you can offer is to make an inquiry rather than offering an opinion. "What do you think of returning to school?" is far more valuable than, "I think that you should go back to school."

Asking questions allows for the dignity of choice and keeps possibilities open. Even if you are pressed for an opinion, you can offer it in the form of a question, such as, "What do you think of staying home tonight?" or, "What if you apologized to her?"

Socrates was convinced that asking questions was the superior way to teach others. He made it the cornerstone of his philosophy. If one of his students asked him about the meaning of life, or anything else, he would reply with a question rather than an answer: "What do *you* think the meaning of life is?" He knew that responding with a question gave the learner room to come up with an innovative reply and to develop the inestimable skill of self-reliance.

Listen without Judgment

I have learned a great deal from listening carefully without judgment.

— ERNEST HEMINGWAY

True listening can only occur when we sweep aside personal preferences and see things from the other person's perspective. Dana, a thirty-five-year-old woman, recounted a story about the power of being heard without judgment and how it changed the course of her life. She was married with a four-year-old child, and her eight-year marriage had been in distress for more than a few years.

Dana met a man at her workplace, a father to three teens and in a strained marriage. Soon they were experiencing the excitement of an intense attraction that she called "out of control" from the onset. With some trepidation, they decided to spend a weekend together.

A few days before she was to depart on the weekend trip with this man, Dana stopped by her mother's house for a short visit. Her mother asked her a few times if anything was upsetting her. Since she had no intention of involving her mother in her love life, she told her that everything was fine. When she was departing, her mother gave her a long hug and said, "Honey, if there is anything bothering you, and you just need someone to listen, I'm here." With those words, Dana broke down and began to cry.

Dana stayed a few more hours and poured out the entire

story to her mother. "I expected my mother to be flabber-gasted, since she was very religious and a firm believer in the sacredness of marriage." Instead, her mother listened keenly without imposing any opinions at all. She didn't even offer any advice. She just listened intently, nodding her head as her daughter spoke, with her chin resting on her hand.

Dana told her mother that she felt she needed to go through with their weekend plans, even though she sensed in her heart that it was not a wise choice. Her mother responded with empathy, and simply said, "I can see that this is a real dilemma for you" and, "I understand what you must be going through right about now."

Dana left confounded, wondering why she had told her mother about the situation at all. After a restless night's sleep, she called off her surreptitious plans. "Because my mother had listened to me without any judgment, I was able to reflect on the price I was paying to live a lie, and I realized that I didn't want to do this to my family or to his. Without the pressure of disapproval or condemnation, I was able to see for myself that I was really seeking a distraction and thrill instead of facing my real problems, which were waiting for me at home."

Dana's mother served as a mirror, giving her the freedom to choose again. She later surprised Dana even more by telling her that she'd been at the same crossroads twenty years earlier. Like her daughter, she stepped away from a potential affair after a mentor was able to listen to her. Consequently, she was able to revive her then-crumbling marriage into a much stronger union that now has passed the forty-year mark.

Dana has been married for more than twelve years and feels that the bond between her and her husband is stronger and more real than before. She still wonders from time to time what her life might be like had she not received the unqualified love and support from her mother in her time of need.

Everybody Needs Somebody to Talk To

It takes a great man or woman to be a good listener.

— CALVIN COOLIDGE

"Everybody needs somebody they can confide in with their whole heart and all of their soul." These wise words of counsel come from psychotherapist Rebecca Miller, who works with troubled teens in Los Angeles County. For more than twenty years, she has helped young adults contending with drug and alcohol abuse, teen pregnancy, felonies, school problems, learning difficulties, sexual abuse, and a variety of family dysfunctions.

Although the backgrounds and circumstances vary from teen to teen, there is one trait shared by all the troubled teens that she consistently observes: they usually don't have any adults whom they can pour out their hearts to. They often feel alone in the world and have a distant or hostile relationship with the adults in their lives. Often things look well enough on the surface, and they may have one or two parents who are under the impression that everything is just fine. These teens usually have same-age buddies they "hang out with," which fills their need to belong to a peer group. But it doesn't fill the need that young adults have to confide and trust in someone in a leadership or authority role.

This void is so pervasive that whole organizations, such

as the Big Brother and Big Sister of America programs, have sprung up nationally to try to alleviate this national epidemic. Rebecca is convinced that people of all ages need to be totally transparent with at least one trustworthy person. In her many years of service to teens, she has found that teens tend to be troubled in direct proportion to their feelings of isolation, shame, abandonment, or poor self-esteem.

The more bottled-up a teen becomes, the more prone to problems and acting out he or she is. The following piece was written by a teen in drug rehabilitation, reflecting the despair he felt when he did not feel heard or understood by the significant people in his world:

LOST

I told my mom I needed to talk,
And she told me she was busy.
I told my teacher I needed help,
And she sent me to the office.
I told my dad I had a problem,
And he told me we'd talk later.
I told my girlfriend I was in trouble,
And she told me she was leaving.
I told my buddy I was freaking out,
And he took me out to get high.
I ran out of people I could talk to,
And I overdosed instead.

The young man who wrote the above poem is now a peer counselor to teens undergoing difficulties. He suggests that parents listen to the nonverbal messages that their children may be sending as well as the verbal ones — to the things that they are doing or not doing as well as to the things they are saying. This includes changes in eating habits, shifts in sleep patterns, clamming up, bouts of anger, changes in grades or study habits at home, secretive behavior, listlessness, nervousness, or any other behavior that might be a cry for help.

If a child or teen can't talk to a family member, reaching out for further help may be called for. Sometimes it's easier for a child to talk about difficulties with a caring professional who listens objectively. Tuning in to a child's words and behavior, and using the four steps of true listening, help to establish an environment of safety and care. In good times and in times of trouble, children of all ages need to be listened to so that they can thrive and move forward.

Exercises

1. Practice the Four Steps of True Listening Often

Using the four steps will prove to be invaluable in every relationship. Start by memorizing the four steps so that they become habitual. Take it on as a project with your children, and practice over meals or while doing tasks. You will discover that listening without offering an opinion is not as easy as it looks, and asking questions rather than giving answers is a discipline that takes time to learn.

Commit to making this way of listening the new standard in your home, and playfully bring each other back to the steps as you self-correct and learn along the way. Stay with it and practice, practice, practice! You will experience nothing less than miraculous shifts in all your interactions.

2. The Safe Confidant Checklist

Make a list of the people in your life with whom you can share everything, with nothing held back — people you feel totally safe being transparent with, who love and accept you without condition. Have your child or teen do the same. Everyone needs to have at least one person to create a "survival list" and at least three people to have a "thrival list." This list is not the same as a social or friendship list and may include professionals, mentors, and guides, as long as they fit the above description.

If you have no one to put on the list, make it a goal to seek out a safe and caring individual or group for you and/or your child. If you do not know where to begin, consider support groups, church groups, or recovery groups. Most of these groups are free, and many promote the ideas mentioned in this chapter.

If your list includes spiritual teachers or close family members who are deceased, it is vitally important that you find at least one to three safe confidants who are alive, warm-blooded, and speak your language! Pets, while clearly a great source of comfort to many, are not to be included on this particular list — people only.

A MESSAGE FROM ALL CHILDREN ABOUT
THE VALUE OF TRUE LISTENING

Dear Parent or Guardian,
The ways that you listen to me
Will help or hinder me.

When you listen to me with judgment,
You teach me to be self-critical.
When you hear me with loving care,
You teach me self-acceptance.

When you try to fix my problems,
You teach me to be dependent.
When you trust in my abilities,
You teach me self-reliance.

So please listen carefully to me,
Including the things I don't say.
I'll feel heard and understood
And able to listen to others.

CHAPTER FOUR

Share Laughter, Play, and Affection

Laugh and have fun with me often,
Be affectionate every day.
I'll play and enjoy my life
And bring more joy to others.

Smiling is contagious! Happy babies have an infectious way of making everyone in their midst smile. Even the sternest of personalities cannot resist lighting up when seeing a smiling or laughing baby. Perhaps it's the wide-eyed look of glee in their eyes, or the amazing way that babies smile, not just with their mouths and faces but with their entire bodies, from the top of their radiant heads to the tips of their exuberant toes.

Go to any public place and observe children over the age of seven, however, and you will find that the older they are, the less they smile. It seems that in Western culture, formal education and seriousness go hand in hand. Children in day care and kindergarten are full of laughter and play, but by the time they finish first grade, their resilience and laughter have usually dramatically declined.

After working with teachers and students for many years as an educational consultant, I've observed that students with teachers who smile and laugh often seem to like school more and to get better grades. Out of this discovery, I was inspired to write a book entitled *The Laughing Classroom* (H J Kramer/New World Library) to encourage teachers of all grade levels to bring more laughter, creativity, and joy into the classroom.

The tendency in children to smile or frown seems to run in families as well. Children with bright, beautiful smiles inevitably come from homes where one or both parents have warm, inviting smiles. Children with pensive, guarded expressions are usually raised in homes with serious adults who are quick to point out what is wrong and slow to find what is going right.

Oprah Winfrey was once asked what she perceived as the most significant image change a person could make in his or her life. Without hesitation, she said, "Changing from a serious expression to a warm smile. There is no single feature more appealing than a smile." A smile gives hundreds of affirming and lighthearted messages without the need to use any words at all. A smile is the perfect nonverbal way of saying, "Welcome. I'm interested in you. I'm happy to see you. I enjoy being with you. I like you. You make me laugh. You're wonderful. I'm fond of you. I love you."

Establish the "Smiling Habit"

Humor is our greatest national resource,
which must be preserved at all costs.

— JAMES THURBER

Children are so receptive to a smile that if a parent could make just one change in a thirty-day period to vastly improve their parenting style, I would suggest smiling more often at their children and offering more hugs and affection. If you are reading this chapter, then consider yourself "elected" to take on the thirty-day smiling challenge with your entire family! Since it takes just three to four weeks to establish a new habit, thirty days is ample time to allow you to witness the magic of bringing more smiles and affection to all the people you interact with every day.

Read the "Big Smiling Oath" at breakfast with your family, and share your stories at dinnertime each evening — and there will be stories! In a world that suffers from far too much seriousness, an unexpected smile, laugh, or hug will bring people, places, and opportunities together in unpredictable ways. Simply by agreeing to smile and laugh more and to give a few hugs a day, you may be inviting more joyful moments into your life than you've had since you were a laughing baby!

THE BIG SMILING OATH

I do unsolemnly swear,
To turn up each side of my mouth,

And to smile as often as possible.
I agree to laugh several times daily,
And to give and receive at least three hugs a day!
I vow to have frequent bouts of silliness,
And more happiness for no reason.
From this day forth,
I promise to laugh long and prosper!

The Significance of Touch and Affection

Touch speaks volumes without uttering a single word!

— ASHLEY MONTAGU

The human need for affection and touch cannot be overemphasized. In the first year of life, it is a known fact that babies can actually die or fall developmentally behind if they are not touched, held, coddled, and loved daily. Toddlers are by nature masters of affection and will readily hug almost anyone if they are receiving love and touch in their home each day. Whether children maintain their natural capacity to reach out and touch depends on how affectionate their parents, guardians, and extended family are.

I was recently having my car serviced at a local shop when the owner's adult son came into the shop to deliver something to his father. The interaction between the two was lively and full of humor. It was almost a novelty to watch a grown father and son taking such joy in each other's presence, and I tried not to be too intrusive as I watched them. When they parted, it was no small parting. They gave one another a hug, followed by a surprising "I love you" exchanged between the two.

I couldn't help but ask the owner about it after his son

strolled out of the shop. "Are you always this affectionate with your son?" I asked inquisitively. "Absolutely," he said with a sparkle in his eye, "with all four of my grown children. I grew up in a stern home with a father who wasn't ever able to tell me he loved me. I decided to do just the opposite with my kids, so I show them as often as possible. There is rarely a day that goes by that I don't tell each one of them that I love them. They are the apples of my eye."

Daniel, an investment banker and father of three, recalls a well-loved neighbor who moved into his neighborhood when Daniel was five. The neighbor's name was Norman, and he was a tall young bachelor who lived in the house next door. Daniel attributes his great capacity to wrestle and play with his children to Norman, since his own father died when he was only four:

> After exchanging a few hellos back and forth over the fence, we learned that our new neighbor was fond of kids — and that he loved to wrestle. What a discovery he was for me and my neighborhood pals, most of whom were starved for this kind of freelance play that our parents were too busy or uptight to even consider.
>
> Before long, we were showing up in his yard to help him mow the lawn or work in the garden. We were good at finding just about any excuse we could think of just to hang around with him. We'd even give up playing baseball to help him rake leaves or pull dandelions, knowing that when we finished, he just might whirl us through the air like airplanes, or toss us one by one into a gigantic heap of raked leaves! It was a thrill to play so hard with an adult who seemed to be having as much fun as we were!

There may be no single form of quality attention that children desire more than affection, hugs, and tactile play. When my daughter, Julia, was a young child, one of her favorite activities was a form of playing that became known as "puppy-piling." A few close family members or friends would huddle close together in a hammock, on a pile of blankets on the floor, or on the rug near a crackling fire and read stories aloud, wrestle, tell jokes together, or just curl up and take a little snooze. For an added twist, Julia would include her guinea pig or her tamed pet rat! The laughter that abounded from this simple form of tactile play has been a source of many happy memories.

Yuerg, a dear friend who was raised in Switzerland, has lasting memories of having his hair stroked by his mother for long periods of time: "She used to talk on the phone for quite a while to distant relatives. Instead of this being a time when my mother was unavailable, it became a bonding time for us. As soon as I could see that she was going to be on the phone for a while, I'd drop whatever I was doing in favor of resting my head in my mother's lap, just to feel her soft hands running through my hair or stroking my head. She never seemed to tire of this, and neither did I, although at some point I became too big to lie my head across her lap!" To this day, this is one of Yuerg's dearest childhood memories.

The Price of Too Much Seriousness

A person without humor is like a wagon without springs —
jolted by every pebble.

— HENRY WARD BEECHER

The three regrets that are the most universal among those in the final chapter of life, reflecting on the years that went by so quickly, are:

1.   I wish I'd shown and expressed love more.

2.   I wish I'd enjoyed life more.

3.   I wish I'd taken more risks.

Despite the universality of these three regrets, most of us take life far too seriously, making mountains out of molehills and trading in our spontaneity, joy, and resilience for routine, fear, and worry. Even if we do realize that worry is a form of "negative meditation" and that 95 percent of what we fear will never come to pass, the human mind seems to have an endless capacity for seriousness. The price of seriousness is steep. Too much seriousness keeps us from opening our hearts, expressing affection, being more creative, and living joyfully.

Thomas, an observant five-year-old boy, was playing with his big sister and pretending to be "Daddy at his desk." He put on some glasses and began to scribble numbers on a piece of paper, while letting out loud sighs and moans. He contorted his face into such a prunish expression that his sister began to laugh out loud. "What are you doing?" she asked through her giggling. "I'm Daddy paying the big pile of bills," Thomas said matter-of-factly, and continued to groan under his breath as he crumpled up some paper and threw it across the floor.

Already, at five years old, he had it wired into his system that paying bills and handling money was an excruciatingly unpleasant task, something he had learned from an expert — his own father, who had the good fortune to overhear his young son imitating him from the next room. He took the matter to heart and became strongly aware of his tendency to be overserious and "prune faced" whenever handling financial matters. He realized that he had been hoodwinked by a long line of prune-faces when it came to money, including his father and grandfather, who had unwittingly passed along the belief that handling money was a serious and miserable matter!

Thomas's father realized how much he was missing, including the appreciation and satisfaction of being able to pay for services rendered — whether for electricity, heat, a home, the use of a car, or the myriad of other things he spent money on each month. Instead of teaching his son about financial responsibility, he had been teaching him that bills are something to resist, resent, and get riled up over, week after week.

The high price he'd been paying for his overserious attitude was negative modeling for his son, misery for himself and his family, and a missed opportunity to teach his son about the privilege of handling money. Because he is now choosing to face the dire effects he's had on his son and family, he is free to choose again and to turn around this old, worn-out habit once and for all.

Anna, a forty-year-old mother, recalls her grim and serious grandmother, who did not know how to smile; when she tried she could only come up with a twisted expression with each side of her mouth turned down:

We all dreaded it when Grandma was scheduled for a visit, because we knew that we'd have to wait on her hand and foot and cater to her many demands — more tea, warmer food, less noise, more attention.

No matter what we did for her, it was never quite right. When the children were playing games or having fun, she would sit on the sidelines feeling neglected. When they laughed just a little too loudly, she would say that the shrillness hurt her ears. She was a female version of Scrooge, complete with cynicism about the holidays and a constant barrage of complaints about her five children, including our dear mother, who had the tolerance of a saint in dealing with her many quirks and demands.

The only time we saw my grandmother amused was when someone was belittling someone else. She seemed to come to life when sarcasm or put-downs were being spoken, just long enough to put in her two cents. The price Grandma paid for her overseriousness was a high one. Her five children were obliging but estranged from her, and her grandchildren felt trepidation around her and found it difficult to converse with her about any topic at all. Because of her serious approach to life, she had sufficiently insulated herself on all sides, and lived a lonely life without a single person who could really say they knew her.

Make the Everyday Moments More Magnificent!

To delight in small things is no small thing!

— THE DALAI LAMA

One of the best ways to bring more humor and play into the house is by making the everyday moments more magical. Throughout my childhood, I loved listening to the humorous and compelling way that my mom read stories aloud to me. She made reading books extraordinary by animating each of the characters with unique voices and gestures. Each time I'd run to sit in her lap and open up a storybook, I'd become enthralled with the performance she put on. The various voices that she used for each of my storybook characters turned reading into an adventure extraordinaire that took place in the privacy of my own home each day!

I not only loved the stories; I had the added benefit of watching my mother enjoy her own dramatic renditions of them too. Diana was truly having fun, not just going through the monotonous motions of reading another boring story to a little kid. It was a delight to see my mom come up with a new gesture or odd sound with each new character. What a wonder it was to see her taking the time to quack like a duck, howl like a wolf, whisper like a tiny elf, or roar like a lion. It personalized each page in a way that is indelibly imprinted in my mind. When I page through my childhood storybooks on occasion, I can still hear all the characters in my mother's many voices.

Every child loves to have a story read aloud. To make the time even more memorable, try bringing the characters to life in your own way. The laughter will last long, and the memories even longer.

Use Humor That Heals, Not Humor That Hurts

A merry heart doeth good like a medicine.

— PROVERBS 17:22

The only rule of thumb regarding humor is to use humor that heals rather than hurts. Humor that heals uplifts children and teaches them more about the principles of love, support, creativity, and compassion. Humor that hurts teaches children about criticism, power struggles, mixed messages, and judgment.

Humor that heals includes the following healthy qualities:

- It takes delight in another.
- It affirms and builds up others.

- It puts no one down.
- It exercises creativity.
- It brings joy and happiness to others.
- It takes a lighthearted view.
- It evokes smiles, laughter, confidence, and well-being.

Children who are raised in homes with humor that heals have happy memories of family and tend to get along much better with their siblings. They remain close to their families as adults and feel safe in the presence of family members, without the burden of ridicule, shaming, or criticism.

Humor that hurts is distinctively different and includes the following qualities:

- It makes fun of another.
- It tears someone or something down.
- It uses put-downs, either indirect or direct.
- It uses cynicism and sarcasm.
- It brings negativity or discouragement to others.
- It takes a biting or bitter view.
- It evokes shame, competition, resentment, or disconnection.

Children who are raised in households with humor that hurts tend to be defensive and guarded around other family members and have mixed feelings about family memories. They tend to be sarcastic and critical with their siblings, and often distance themselves from their families as adults to protect themselves from more ridicule, shaming, and criticizing.

The Power of Lightheartedness under Fire

It takes a long time to become young.

— PABLO PICASSO

It has been said that the true test of humor is found not in times of joy, but in times of adversity. One of the most inspiring true stories about the use of humor under fire involves a retired couple, Ralph and Emma. Throughout their marriage they had always wanted to take an extended European trip. After raising five children, they happily bid farewell to their family to fulfill their lifelong dream in celebration of their fiftieth anniversary.

They left their children in charge of watching over their wonderful home, which had been recently remodeled to their delight and satisfaction. Since their parents' itinerary was quite full, visiting five countries in six weeks, the children assured them that there was no need to be in touch and that they would look forward to hearing all about the trip when they returned.

A few days before they returned, a terrible fire broke out in the canyon area, and all the surrounding neighbors were evacuated from their homes. Tragically, Ralph and Emma's beloved home, like so many others in the area, was burnt to the ground, along with all the beautiful fruit trees, shrubs, and burgeoning gardens that had been Ralph's pride and joy. Since the two lovebirds were having the time of their life and not exactly on schedule, their children were unable to reach them directly to inform them of the heartbreaking news — they had lost everything, including their art collection, furniture, clothing, personal and family memorabilia, and even their cars, which were now hollowed-out clumps of charred metal in what once had been the garage.

When Ralph and Emma flew into the airport a day early, there was nothing they wanted more than to sink into the comfort of their wonderful home and catch up on some much-needed rest. Full of laughter and chatter, they held hands as they drove out of the airport parking lot and toward their home in the canyon. Instead of being bombarded by the radio and local news, they played Beethoven's "Ode to Joy," which reminded them of the sweeping countryside of southern France they had bicycled through just one week before.

Within miles of home, they began to witness the darkened sky, burnt trees, and fallen ashes along the canyon roads and hillsides. Ralph had a sick feeling in the pit of his stomach, and Emma couldn't seem to catch her breath. Their silence was thick in the air as they drove up the winding road and saw the gutted-out vestiges of homes scattered across the blackened canyon. They savored the final moments they had left to hope and pray that their home had been spared before they drove around the last curved road that would bring their home into view.

As they made the turn, Ralph immediately turned off the music and stopped the car. Emma gasped in horror and buried her face in Ralph's shoulder. Ralph gripped Emma's hand tightly, and the two of them said nothing for what seemed like a very long time. Ralph slowly got out of the car and stepped onto the ashen grounds, feeling weak in the knees and overcome with a shaking that gripped his entire body.

Emma followed suit and walked trembling toward the ruins that had been home sweet home for so long. Each of them took in the devastating sights and smells, trying to comprehend that everything was gone forever, had quite literally gone up in smoke. They hugged one another, cried, hugged some more, and intermittently sat together as Emma kept repeating, "Oh, Ralph, it's gone — everything we've ever had is just gone!"

Then, the unexpected happened...a defining moment that would change everything. Ralph trudged over to the top of the canyon, where the damage was in full view, and looked out for a long time. Then, he began to chuckle — first a quiet cackle, which quickly moved into a deep and full-bellied laugh. "What is it?" Emma asked incredulously, "Tell me, Ralph." As he extended his arms out to his wife, he said through his laughter, "Oh Emma, don't you see? It's just a test. Today our home and belongings; tomorrow our bodies! Someday, not so long from now, we will be leaving our whole lives, as we have known them. This is just a warm-up. Consider us fortunate to have an opportunity for a dress rehearsal!"

Something came over Emma as she heard his words, and she was able to get a glimpse of the gift within the ruins. She embraced her husband as they laughed and cried some more. "Our true home is not this, Emma," Ralph continued, "It's the love that we have in our hearts that no fire can ever destroy. I still have you, my love, and even a single day that God has granted me on this earth, and with you, is worth more than all the houses this world could ever hold!"

Before contacting their loved ones, Ralph went to the car and turned Beethoven's "Ode to Joy" back on. Extending his hand to his wife, he smiled through his tears and said, "I was wondering if my forever bride would be willing to have this dance?" Emma reached out for his hand, and they began to dance on the concrete slab that had once been their patio. She embraced her husband and shared a dance with him as he swept her through the ash and ruin.

Ralph and Emma had many months ahead of legal paperwork, temporary housing, rebuilding, and emotional adjusting, but they never lost sight of the lightheartedness that had inspired Ralph amid the biggest loss of their lives. His "grace under fire" was an inspiration to his family, friends, and the entire community. "We're still here," Ralph said in the months following, "and we still have each other. Not even a devastating fire can keep us from realizing how few things in life really matter other than love."

Exercises

1. Take On the Thirty-Day Smile Challenge

Take on the thirty-day smiling challenge as a family, and share the results each night at the dinner table. Be sure to include one another in your hugging quotas each day. At the end of thirty days, go on a special family outing to celebrate your accomplishment.

2. Take a "Seriousness" Inventory

List all the things that you are taking far too seriously in your life and in your interactions with others. Take a serious look at the price you are paying for too much seriousness in three major areas of your life (such as finances, housework, and exercise). Talk with family members and friends about how you can lighten up, and ask for gentle reminders if you fall back into old patterns.

3. Choose to Be Lighthearted under Fire

Think of a time when you or someone you know was able to be "lighthearted under fire." How did it affect the circumstances, and what kind of lasting impact did it have on you? Discuss these questions and more with family members, and be as honest as possible.

A MESSAGE FROM ALL CHILDREN ABOUT
PLAY AND AFFECTION

Dear Parent or Guardian,
Your lighthearted or serious attitude
Casts glory or gloom on my world.

When you take life too seriously,
You teach me to be uptight.
When you take things in stride,
You teach me to be lighthearted.

When you are unaffectionate,
You teach me to be distant.
When you nurture me with touch,
You teach me to be affectionate.

So please be more lighthearted,
And smile and laugh more often.
I'll enjoy just being near you
And develop a sense of humor.

CHAPTER FIVE

Give Acknowledgment and Show Appreciation

Acknowledge me often,
And tell me when you appreciate me.
I'll know that I am worthy
And learn to acknowledge others.

We all desire to give and receive more acknowledgment, even if we don't realize how deep this desire runs. Out of habit, most of us don't consistently acknowledge others or express appreciation for all the wonderful things we so often take for granted. Yet when we express to someone what a difference he or she makes in our lives, we sense that we have just contributed something very significant.

Practice the Three Big A's:
Acknowledgment, Appreciation, and Awe

Appreciation is a wonderful thing.
It makes what is excellent in others belong to us as well.

— FRANÇOIS VOLTAIRE

Practicing the Three Big A's (acknowledgment, appreciation, and awe) deepens intimacy, uplifts the spirit, and improves our relationships. To *acknowledge* is to take notice of a wonderful quality or contribution in someone or something. "I want to acknowledge how generously you give of yourself to others" and "You really have a talent for playing music" are both examples of taking notice and commenting on admirable qualities in another.

To *appreciate* is to grasp the nature and worth of something or someone and to express gratitude: "I really appreciate the quality time you put into this project" or "I love you so much. What would I do without you?" exemplify the gift of appreciation.

To be in *awe* is to have reverence or veneration inspired by something magnificent or sublime: "Look at the brilliant sky tonight. Isn't it beautiful?" or "Watching you grow into such a caring person is a real inspiration to me" are examples of sharing awe.

Those who have the good fortune of growing up with someone who expresses the Three Big A's have a wealth of fond memories and magnificent moments to savor. They are more likely to express the Three A's to the important people in their lives and to have more joy in life's small and great moments.

No Act of Appreciation Is Ever Too Small

The deepest desire in the human being
is the craving to be appreciated.

— RALPH WALDO EMERSON

To be appreciated may be one of the deepest desires of all residing in every human being. There is not a race or tribe in the world that does not create ritual to express appreciation for others. In our modern-day culture, our appreciation ceremonies include everything from birthday parties, humanitarian awards, the Oscars, and the Nobel Peace Prize. As important as appreciation is, most people are sorely lacking the appreciation they would like from their families, friends, and associates.

Three teens and their mother were celebrating their father's fortieth birthday, with the intention to make it especially memorable. They asked him a very important birthday question: "Dad, how can we show our appreciation for you more in the next year?" Duane was taken by surprise and responded, "This question is the best present of all. There is something I would like more of. When I come home from work at night, everyone's busy or scattered to the winds doing their own thing. I sometimes wish that someone was there to say hello after a long day at work. If you could greet me or visit for a minute or two when I arrive home, it would be great. I don't expect this every day, maybe once or twice a week."

Duane's wife and teens decided to respond with a flair to show him how much they cared. They began taking turns greeting Duane at the door almost daily. The first day, his fifteen-year-old daughter greeted him with his favorite hot green tea and slippers. The next day, Duane's thirteen-year-old son turned off the television and came over to talk to his dad about his day and the basketball game that was on.

As the days went by, family members continued to greet him, give him a hug, or ask him about his day. Occasionally, he was greeted by two or more of his children. One of his favorite ways to be welcomed was by his wife, who would sit him down in his favorite chair and give him a shoulder massage while putting on some of his favorite music. Since Duane spent a lot of time on a computer at work, this was relaxing as well as nurturing.

As small an act of appreciation as this was, Duane considered it one of the most meaningful things his family ever did for him. Small gestures of appreciation do so much to make the people we care most about in our lives feel special and cared for. No act of appreciation is ever too small.

Catch Yourself Doing Something Good

*It is only by finding the good in ourselves
that we can ever hope to see it in others.*

— HENRY DAVID THOREAU

As a life coach, I am often surprised by how difficult it is for clients to acknowledge themselves or to talk about what's going right in their lives. At the beginning of our weekly sessions, we acknowledge five "wins" that have occurred in the last week. In the beginning it is frequently a struggle to come up with five. But once the process gets going, it gets easier, and sometimes clients mention ten or even fifteen wins as the weeks pass.

The five-wins exercise celebrates what is going right rather than emphasizing what is going wrong. The selected wins don't have to be major or monumental. "Yesterday I got up early to exercise, and accomplished my fitness goal before 8 A.M." might be a big daily accomplishment, and "I was patient with my son even though he has been really cranky lately" may be a bigger achievement than it appears.

On occasion, the wins shared are more significant: "I finished writing the final chapter of my book ahead of schedule" or "I've successfully completed my six-month rehabilitation program." Equally significant are the quiet victories no one might ever know of, such as, "Instead of beating myself up for not getting enough done, I took a half-day off and went to the art museum to get some perspective" or "My meditations are more meaningful now, and I see what a difference they're making in my life."

Since most of us realize the importance of finding the good, why do we so often find it difficult to focus on our achievements? Perhaps it's because most of us were raised with so many negative beliefs and mind-sets. Some research indicates that children hear up to fifteen hundred negative statements for every thirty positives. Can you imagine the impact this has on all of us if the statistics are even partially true?

Because of this dynamic, I ask most clients to write their five wins in a daily journal. This establishes the constructive habit of reflecting on achievements at the end of the day, which is definitely not something most of us are accustomed to doing. People surprise themselves with how many wins they have accomplished in a single day, however small some of them may appear.

As clients become comfortable and familiar with celebrating their wins, they are invited to take on the *advanced five-wins practice,* which is to take one or two mini-breaks during the day to briefly reflect on wins that have happened in the last few hours. You can do this while driving, having a meal, performing everyday tasks, or sitting at a desk. Even on the most challenging days, you will receive a burst of energy after naming a few wins. "I got up early; I set up the overdue dental appointment for my son; I took the time to prepare a healthy breakfast; I listened to a friend in need; and I put another $500 into a lucrative investment — all before noon!" By doing this, we begin to see the cup of life as half-full rather than half-empty, and we have a growing sense of self-respect.

Developing the skill of self-acknowledgment cannot be overestimated. Since many of us have an active inner critic owing to the excess of negativity we've been exposed to, we may find ourselves dealing with the critic's accusations — "Why can't I ever get this right?...I'll never figure this out.... No one else is as stuck as I am.... What is wrong with me?...Maybe I just don't have what it takes." The capacity to find the good in ourselves, and to appreciate all that we do on our own behalf, may be the best antidote to the inner critic. With enough momentum, a consistent look at what is going right may put the inner critic out of business entirely!

Teaching children the skill of acknowledgment is as significant as teaching them the Three R's (reading, writing, and arithmetic). Children who know how to acknowledge themselves and others are less dependent on the approval of others and have more resources in taking risks and being authentic. They exude more overall confidence than children who depend entirely on others to receive accolades and acknowledgment. Imagine a third grader who can come home from school after a hard day and say, "It was a tough day, but I guess I did have a few wins. I made it to the bus on time in the rain, I got a B on the English test, I met a new kid at school over lunch, I wore my new T-shirt that I bought with my own money, and I didn't get mad when Travis tried to pick a fight." Consider starting a "five-wins board" where children can write and post their wins daily, or encourage them to start a wins book of their own.

Catch Others Doing Something Good

A compliment given brings ten back.

— JAPANESE PROVERB

People are so accustomed to being confronted about what they're doing wrong, that to make a big deal when we catch them doing something right can be a surprising and rewarding experience. When my daughter, Julia, was a little girl, there were times when she would be in the middle of playing or doing her homework and I would call her name out of the blue: "Julia, come quick!" She would come bounding down the stairs with a concerned look on her face, only to be duped by an unexpected acknowledgment. I might pick her up or give her a kiss and say, "Hooray, my girl cleaned the sink. Double hooray, she remembered to sweep the floor too!"

You can probably imagine the results. She'd do her chores more willingly and sometimes ahead of schedule, in anticipation of receiving that kind of acknowledgment. When she'd finish her homework, she knew that she could probably expect a clichéd phrase from me, such as, "Good for you, genius!" Although some of my lines were silly and canned, to this day they can still bring a smile to her face.

Vincent, a senior vice president at a large Internet company, decided to take up the habit of catching his employees doing something good. He began by creating "white slips," which were given out to acknowledge excellence of any kind. Previous to this, they only had "red slips," which were written to point out something wrong. Vince decided that he would give everyone in his division one white slip a month — no small task, given his busy schedule. Within weeks, productivity went up, sick days were down, and there was more camaraderie among colleagues than ever. He had the best surprise birthday party ever, thrown by his employees. They presented him with a large wrapped box that was filled with white slips — one or more from each of his cohorts, who thanked him in many ways for being such a great boss.

Alicia and Derek were a young married couple who were strongly considering getting a divorce over what amounted to a series of small, inconsiderate habits rather than any irreconcilable differences. I took them on as clients and gave them some assignments from my intensive coaching program entitled "Relationship 911." I suggested they take three weeks to catch each other doing as many good things as possible before throwing in the towel. In addition, I asked them to write love notes to each other — at least one a day to express compliments and to acknowledge what they appreciated about one another — the more intimate and original the better.

Best of all, they had to continually surprise one another — with a note tucked under a pillow, a card hidden under a plate, a snack with a small note wrapped around it, or even a small token or gift hidden in a medicine cabinet, tool area, or kitchen cupboard. The idea was to bring back a child-like spirit of surprise and play, along with acknowledgment and appreciation. In addition, they both agreed to stay away entirely from the Three Deadly C's — criticizing, complaining, or condemning over anything for a whole month.

Regarding the problems that needed to be addressed, I asked them to write them down using the "plus approach." Rather than just pointing out what was wrong, they agreed to "plus" any challenging situation by offering a solution. Instead of saying, "You didn't pay the credit card bill on time, and now we have a penalty to pay," it might read, "I'd like to plus our bill paying by starting a file system that reminds us to pay each bill one week ahead of schedule to avoid penalties. I'm willing to set this system up and ask that you help to follow through on it. What do you think?" What a difference! The old blaming approach triggers shame and a sense of separation, while the plus approach is fresh, innovative, and opens up new possibilities.

In less than a week, Alicia and Derek were amazed by the shift in the quality of their communication. They never realized how much they thought and talked about what wasn't right. They were both surprised by the childlike joy they took in giving and receiving the unexpected notes and small gifts, which had been missing almost entirely from their relationship. They were learning so much about one another that they didn't previously know. Derek didn't realize how much Alicia thrilled in hearing his hearty laugh until he read that in one of her surprise notes. Alicia never knew how much it meant to Derek when she read to him at night, until he took the time to tell her in a card. It is an interesting phenomenon to witness — when a family atmosphere is filled with safety, play, and acknowledgment, life becomes an endless adventure rather than a repetitive grind.

After Derek and Alicia's initial three-week period, they still had challenges to move through, but the turnaround in their marriage was evident to all. As soon as they committed to halting the destructive habit of zooming in on the negative, their relationship changed course. "We got much more than a repair job," Derek later said. "We went through an overhaul!"

Acknowledgment Do's and Don'ts

I have just one thing to say regarding compliments —
thank-you, and same to you!

— VICTOR BORGE

Whoever thought that guidelines might be needed for something as wonderful as acknowledging others? Yet as we all know, there are some who say nice words while sending a negative message, and those who say something kind just to get a certain outcome. For these reasons and more, you may find the following guidelines useful.

Acknowledgment Do's

The following do's increase the rapport in your relationship with others:

- Do emphasize character over appearance. That will stick the longest!

- Do acknowledge others in ways that mean the most to them. This shows true caring.

- Do say all the things that matter most. You'll be grateful that you did.

- Do be sincere when you give compliments. People sense the difference.

- Do acknowledge loved ones often. It is nutrition for the soul.

- Do speak only well of people in the presence of others. It is deeply affirming.

- Do let others know how they enhance your life. It's the ultimate compliment.

Acknowledgment Don'ts

The following don'ts decrease the rapport in your relationships with others:

- Don't overemphasize success or achievement. Doing so can cause pressure or tension.

- Don't be embarrassing or inappropriate. Be sensitive to the person and setting.

- Don't use a compliment to get something you want. Ultimately, it never works.

- Don't be overly sentimental, doting, or wordy. Keep it sweet and simple.

- Don't be insincere in any way, for any reason. People are too smart for that.

- Don't acknowledge someone just to win his or her affection. The price is too high.

- Don't compliment one person and leave out another. This is divisive instead of unifying.

The Transforming Power of Acknowledgment

The willingness to see the good in another is the first step toward creating harmony.

— WILLIAM JAMES

The simple act of acknowledgment can potentially transform even the most persistent of human conflicts. Marla, a single mother with thirteen-year-old twins, was having a difficult time dealing with sibling rivalry. "Jason and Janelle always seem to be at each other's throats, bickering back and forth almost constantly" were the words she used to describe how tense the situation had become. She wanted to put a stop to this unnerving behavior as soon as possible since it was putting a strain on the entire family. Her six-year-old daughter sometimes cried and left the room when her older siblings argued. Marla decided to initiate the practice of acknowledgment at the dinner table each night.

At first the twins were utterly resistant to the idea and could only come up with sarcastic comments about one another. After several days of realizing their mother was serious, they slowly moved from ridiculous remarks such as "I like how late you sleep on the weekends so that I don't have to deal with you as much" to more authentic comments such as "I appreciate that you've taught me to use the computer." "You're cool to my friends when they stop by," Jason told his sister, "you talk to them when you don't have to."

Over time, the acknowledgments became more personal. "You always know what to do when someone is down," Jason told Janelle one evening. "You are one of the funniest people I've ever known," Janelle told Jason in return, which floored him since he always thought she hated his wacky sense of humor!

Before long, this single mother of three watched her teens building what appeared to be a budding friendship. The next year, when they went into the ninth grade, Jason and Janelle were "watching each other's backs" and able to "talk about anything." Their constant competition and nagging criticism had transformed into a supportive sibling relationship. What a great relief and joy it was for Marla and her family to witness. She took a risk and introduced something new into the household, despite the initial resistance, and it paid off in ways that exceeded her expectations.

Acknowledgment has the power to heal many wounds, including those incurred from years of verbal and physical abuse. Alex, a young man of thirty, had so much more potential than he was able to bring forth for the first twenty-eight years of his life. He was raised in a dysfunctional home with unstable, addictive parents. Between neglect and physical abuse, his talents went unnoticed, and he was ridiculed for his weaknesses. Alex was intermittently subjected to strict punishment, including beatings and deprivation throughout his childhood and was tormented by cruel comments and name-calling. He was frequently called "loser," "lazy dog," and "stupid idiot."

Despite these setbacks, he was a very intelligent young boy who excelled in math, science, and English. He was naturally athletic and became something of a sports star in grade school. Yet over time, the derogatory comments left him so numb that he lost his ambition to succeed in sports or school subjects. As a teen, he let his many talents slip through the cracks and began to drink in excess, leaving him restless and lost much of the time.

As he matured, Alex married a woman who was raised with similar abuse, which they became proficient at using against one another whenever they argued. For more than ten years, this talented young man worked at a mediocre job for a meager salary, reinforcing his sense of worthlessness. His tumultuous marriage eventually ended in a messy divorce, which only added to his sense of failure. Alex was heading nowhere fast and resigned to being in survival mode, working a lackluster job just to make ends meet. He spent his days working and his nights drinking with his host of "good old boy" cronies.

Despite these troubles, he had a heart of gold and an incredible sense of compassion, which many people were drawn to, including a wonderful young woman named Larissa. It wasn't until Alex met Larissa, who became his second wife, that his true nature began to flourish. When Larissa entered his life, her love and support were like oxygen in his suffocating circumstances. Larissa had received a lot of praise and acknowledgment in her life, and she had the ability to see the talents in others.

When Larissa met Alex, she recognized that he was incredibly special, just a bit "misdirected," as she wisely put it. She saw his unique gifts and expressed her confidence in his ability to succeed. Whenever he expressed self-doubt or self-criticism, she invited him to look at himself through "new eyes." Naturally, he mirrored her affections, and their fondness blossomed into true love. Within two years, they married, and Alex embarked on a career venture that enabled him to use more of his people skills and innate intelligence. As an entrepreneur, he created a new career that reflected the innovation that had always been within him.

Alex felt that he owed all his success to his beloved wife for her consistent, uplifting love and acknowledgment. In her presence, he felt unstoppable. She was quick to compliment him and never lost sight of his potential. For the first time, he was able to work hard and to use all his talents to reach the top of his field. He now lives in a beautiful home with his loving wife and their growing son and daughter, whom he affectionately calls his "shooting stars."

Through the power of love and acknowledgment, a young woman with a vision was able to inspire a talented but misdirected man out from under his limitations and into his greatness. Imagine the profound effects of acknowledging your child in this way each day. There is no greater love than this.

Exercises

1. Practice the Five-Wins Exercise Daily

Make it a practice to keep a wins journal (and encourage your children to do the same), and record five wins each night before going to sleep. You'll be surprised by how many things you'll catch yourself doing right, and you will fall asleep with a sense of self-appreciation. Share your wins with at least one trusted person each week. As a family, share five wins each day at the diner table, or keep a win board in the kitchen to write down daily wins for all to see and acknowledge.

2. Establish the Three Big A's

Express *acknowledgment, appreciation,* and *awe* each day. It can lift the worst of moods, lend perspective, and shower those around you with positive energy and inspiration.

~

A MESSAGE FROM ALL CHILDREN ABOUT
THE POWER OF ACKNOWLEDGMENT

Dear Parent of Guardian,
You hold the key to building me up
Or tearing me down
With the power of your words.

When you emphasize what I'm doing wrong,
You teach me to be self-critical.
When you focus on what I'm doing right,
You teach me to be self-accepting.

When you criticize me or put me down,
You teach me self-condemnation.
When you praise or acknowledge me,
You teach me to be a better person.

So please take the time to acknowledge me
And to catch me doing something good.
My behavior will improve dramatically,
And my self-esteem will soar.

CHAPTER SIX

Use Positive Discipline with Respect

Teach me to be disciplined,
And correct me with kindness.
I'll lead a life of dignity,
With the pride of self-respect.

All children need consistency. Everyone who has worked or lived with children knows that they function best on a schedule that balances rest, work, play, learning, regular meals, and quality time with adults and their peers. Aristotle said, "We are what we repeatedly do. Excellence, then, is not an act, but a habit." Children seem to thrive most when provided with clear rules and healthy boundaries. These give children the security of structure rather than the chaos of an environment that can't be counted on.

When my daughter, Julia, was young, she had a resistance to taking naps that let up only on the rare days when she was too exhausted to do anything else but give in. As a baby, she would cry for as long as she could hold out when I put her in her crib. As a toddler, she would sometimes stand up in her crib and raise her small clenched fists above her head to express her utter dismay at being removed from the excitement of her day to do something as mundane as taking a nap. Yet, as every adult knows, the naps that she resisted with all her might were also her saving grace — so necessary for her rest, growth, and well-being.

What if I'd decided that it was just too much effort to go through this every day and done away with naps to avoid the power struggle? It may have been easier in the short run, but it would have been a detriment to my young daughter. She'd have fallen into an overtired period most days and possibly become irritable around others. How many exhausted, cranky kids can remember to cooperate, share with others, or to say please and thank you? She would have fallen asleep in random places, without having a quiet, designated place to rest and to receive the consistency her little system so direly needed. She would also sense instinctively that she was somehow out of sync with life. The chaos of it all would have fast become more of a burden than a benefit for everyone involved.

Karen, a young single parent with a toddler, wasn't raised in an orderly household and didn't have any idea how to create consistency with her young son, Brian. He was allowed to stay up each night until he fell asleep, which was frequently as late as eleven or twelve o'clock. Brian was allowed to eat whatever he wanted at any time and often went into the refrigerator and grabbed anything that was available. He was well aware that all he had to do to get his mother's attention was to pull on her legs and whine relentlessly, which he often did while she was on the phone, since she'd give him candy or treats to keep him quiet. When Brian was upset, his cry was so shrill that it made everyone in the area cringe, especially his mother, who would do just about anything to quiet him down.

Karen's living room resembled a mini–day care center, since Brian's toys filled every part of the room and were rarely picked up. Needless to say, Brian was already considered "behaviorally challenged" at the local day care center and was already finding it difficult to follow the school rules at the tender age of three. What Brian was really crying out for were boundaries, a schedule, and a consistent environment he could count on. His social ineptness had more to do with the chaos and inconsistency at home than anything else. Had Karen understood how to create a home that modeled the twelve signs listed below, Brian may have had a very different school experience.

Twelve Signs of a Healthy, Consistent Environment

Consistency begets self-mastery.

— FRIEDRICH NIETZSCHE

A child who lives in a consistent, reliable environment with fair rules that are understood by all is a balanced, cooperative child. Use the following checklist to take an inventory of your home or the home you were raised in as a child. Use it to explore what level of consistency you have currently established in your home. Each number that you check is progress toward creating a more balanced, harmonious home.

1. _____ Nutritious meals served at scheduled times, frequently shared as a family

2. _____ Nutritious snacks with limits on sweets and treats

3. _____ Regular bedtime hours, especially during the school week

4. _____ Curfew on weeknights and weekends appropriate to age

5. _____ Consistent household chores that are age appropriate

6. _____ Reasonable cleanliness and order kept in the home most of the time

7. _____ Respectful manners and positive communication among all family members

8. _____ Homework or chores completed on schedule with good follow-through

9. _____ Reasonable limits on television, telephone, the Internet, or video games

10. _____ Sibling respect regarding feelings, needs, differences, and privacy

11. _____ Quality time with parents and with the family as a whole on a regular basis

12. _____ Clear rules and agreements established with fair, natural consequences

Twelve Signs of an Unhealthy, Inconsistent Environment

Without consistency, there is no moral strength.

— JOHN J. OWEN

Go through the following checklist to explore what areas of your home environment need improvement. Each number you mark is an area of chaos or unpredictability to remedy. Use this list as a guideline, with the intention of eliminating checks in all twelve areas over time:

1. _____ Meals served at random times, without sitting down to eat together

2. _____ Nonnutritious snacks, sweets, and treats available anytime

3. _____ Erratic bedtime hours during the school week and weekends

4. _____ Curfew inappropriate to age (too early or too late), or no curfew at all

5. _____ Household chores that are age inappropriate (too few or too many)

6. _____ Clutter, chaos, junk, filth, or disorder in the home most of the time

7. _____ Poor manners or disrespectful communication among family members

8. _____ No regular homework time or accountability/follow-through on homework

9. _____ No limits on the use of television, telephone, the Internet, and video games

10. _____ Sibling disrespect regarding feelings, needs, differences, or privacy

11. _____ Quality time between parents and children irregular or nonexistent

12. _____ Unclear rules or agreements with random punishments or no consequences

The Tyranny of Too Much Freedom

No one is free who is not master of himself.

— WILLIAM SHAKESPEARE

Some of the most persistent and unproductive habits that people carry with them for a lifetime have their roots in childhood patterns of poor self-discipline. I see this often when working with clients, such as forty-two-year-old Malia, who was seeking relief from her lifelong habits of avoidance and procrastination:

> When I was a child, and throughout my teen years, my family had a nickname for me — "the putzer." I'm not sure where this less-than-complimentary name came from, but I lived up to it by being the best procrastinator in the entire house, able to veer off track in the middle of any task, and taking what seemed like forever to complete my chores. I could start a list of what amounted to thirty minutes' worth of tasks, and still not be done eight hours later!
>
> I recall spending countless Saturdays piddling the day away before completing my chores. Between my vivid imagination and my capacity to be easily distracted, the simple act of vacuuming the living room might be interrupted by

my dancing to music, making a few phone calls, fiddling in a drawer, and taking a few play breaks with my little brother. No wonder it took me hours to finish a few simple tasks on my list!

Most frustrating of all was the way my parents treated my inordinate capacity to procrastinate. They simply let me do it, without providing any structure or consequences for not getting things done in a reasonable time frame. Their philosophy was, "If it takes her all day, then she's wasted the day away, and she'll have to live with that!" The trouble with this approach was that I never did learn the lesson they hoped I would. All I learned was that I was deficient, or even defective, and that it was probably hopeless.

Despite the shame that followed each of my weekly episodes, it only got worse as I matured. I remember as a preteen cringing as my older sister would come back from a fun day of outings with a look of shock on her face as she'd say, "Are you still doing your housework?" My parents often checked in with one another and said, "Well, how many hours did she waste today?" I can't say that this was the most constructive message my parents ever gave me!

By the time I was in high school, my procrastination problem had migrated to several more areas of my life. I was frequently late for school and often received warning slips and detentions for tardiness. I became adept at cramming all night for tests and going without sleep, because my capacity to put things off instead of studying was so well developed. I was so often late for my part-time job in my senior year of high school that I was almost fired, and more than once.

Needless to say, this menacing habit has trailed after me into my adult life. My husband and children have contended with my tardiness for years, since I still have a great capacity to put things off. Instead of getting to my paperwork and mail in a timely way, I've often left clutter piles trailed throughout the house — on the desk, on the counters, in the closets, and in the garage. I've often been late returning phone calls, showing up for appointments, or attending social functions. When my brother got married last year, my husband and teens were so sure I'd be late for the wedding, they drove in a separate car to avoid the embarrassment of walking in late with me. That was a big wake-up call for me, especially because I was late for my brother's wedding, despite my frantic attempts to be on time.

Recently, I hired a professional organizer and joined a support group to receive help as I begin to unravel these insidious habits and to establish a new way of living. I realize it's never too late to learn the skills of scheduling, punctuality, and task completion. The tyranny of too much freedom has cost me so very much. I've finally reached the point of knowing that "enough is enough" and that there's no turning back.

I no longer blame my parents for giving me so much rope to hang myself with. But I do encourage every parent I know to teach the vital skills of time management and task completion to their children. Giving kids reasonable time frames to complete their tasks, with fair consequences that are known ahead of time, is mandatory for their growth and development.

If a child doesn't finish morning dishes by 11 A.M., and that's the agreed-on time, then having them do the morning and lunch dishes together makes sense. If a child wakes up late and doesn't make the bed before going to school, having them make all the beds the next day will assure that this doesn't happen very often. Kids may not like them in the moment, but if these consequences are implemented consistently, the results will benefit the children for a lifetime. Take it from me, a "recovering putzer" and one extra-late bloomer!

Healthy Self-Discipline: A Vital Skill

Self-discipline is the golden key; without it,
you cannot be happy.

— MAXWELL MALTZ

Every parent wants their children to have confidence and good self-esteem. A child who feels loved and cared for develops a great sense of worth, but true esteem comes from a balance of being loved and cared for and the experience of self-mastery, which comes from having strong self-discipline. There are few skills more significant to a child's confidence level than the capacity to exercise self-discipline.

Self-discipline will carry a child through the many choices and challenges that must be faced daily: completing difficult homework when play looks much more appealing, rolling out of bed when it's still dark for early-morning sports practice, or curbing one's words out of respect for another when anger erupts. In a recent survey conducted by Loyola University, poor self-discipline was rated as the number-one trait associated with failure in school. Below are seven major qualities to cultivate in you and your child:

Seven Qualities of a Well-Disciplined Child

1. *Orderly:* keeps room or personal area clean and in order most of the time

2. *Responsible:* completes work or chores on time, reliable in general

3. *Organized:* able to follow a schedule, list, or plan appropriate to age

4. *Punctual:* able to be on time and to complete tasks within a time frame

5. *Mood literate:* ability to temper moods and express emotions in appropriate ways

6. *Cooperative:* able to see both sides of an issue; a win-win team player

7. *Respectful:* treats people of all ages with respect; polite, helpful, and caring

Redirect Misbehavior
with Firm Kindness

*Correct children with respect and kindness
and they will respond back with respect and kindness —
if not immediately, then surely in time.*

— THE DALAI LAMA

At a local day care center, I recently observed a hurried parent rushing to pick up her overtired four-year-old son, who had spent a long day in the company of more than twenty-five four-year-olds. When he saw his mother finally arrive with a stressed-out look on her face, he yanked a toy out of the hands of a nearby child and proceeded to hit the child over the head with the toy and then take a run for it. His mother's knee-jerk reaction was to dash over and slap her son on the hand while prying the toy from his clenched grip saying, "Brett, what is wrong with you? That is so rude — give it back and say you're sorry right now!"

As you can guess, this only aggravated his acting out,

which went from bad to worse as he ran to hide under a table and began to kick and cry. In her reactive state, his mother slapped him and proceeded to shame him in front of his peers, even though she was the one who had arrived late. Had it occurred to her to apologize to him for her tardiness, giving him a big hug and having a snack on hand in case he was hungry?

By focusing on his inappropriate behavior and reprimanding him for it, she was reinforcing the negative. On top of that, she was modeling the very behavior she was punishing him for by berating him and telling him how rude he was. Imagine how many friends she'd lose if she responded in a similar fashion when one of the adults in her world did something she didn't like. Where did anyone ever get the idea that it's okay to treat children with disrespect when no healthy adult would stand for it?

Imagine how much more effective this frazzled mother might have been if she'd taken her son aside and simply apologized for her tardiness and offered a little empathy by saying, "I'm so sorry, Brett. You must be tired and frustrated waiting so long for me, and I'll bet you're hungry too. I brought a little snack for you, and as soon as you apologize to Paul and give the toy back to him, we can go home."

Brett would have benefited greatly from his mother's apology, which would have made it easier to look at his own inappropriate behavior. With kindness and respect in the mix, Brett would have probably apologized without a fuss. Using firm kindness and respect when redirecting misbehavior teaches a child self-respect as well as respect for others.

Curb Destructive Behavior
in Constructive Ways

*Self-control may be developed in precisely the same manner
as we tone up a weak muscle — by little exercises day by day.*

— W. G. JORDAN

Most children go through at least a phase or two of acting out
or some form of misbehavior. For some, it happens during
the toddler years. Others are wonderfully cooperative until
they enter puberty, when their inner turmoil heightens.
Some parents rave that their child took almost no effort to
raise until he or she turned sixteen. And some kids face a
challenge transitioning into young adulthood and successfully leaving home. No matter what the age of your child, it
is important to address misbehavior as soon as it appears. The
key is to do the correcting in caring and constructive ways.

The most significant message that parents can send children of any age is, "Even though your behavior needs improvement, I love you now and always." Robin, a devoted
mother of two children, recounts the difficulty her family went
through when their adopted son began to act out in some dis-
turbing ways. By focusing on curbing his misbehavior con-
structively, she and her husband were able to come up with
some highly effective and creative ways to remedy the problem:

When my husband and I found out we couldn't have any
more children after our daughter, Emily, was born, we
decided to wait a few years and then adopt. When our
daughter turned ten, we were blessed with the opportunity to adopt a four-year-old boy from Korea. As much as
we loved our new addition to the family, we soon learned

that Kent had a few behavior problems that really had us baffled.

After living with us for a couple of months, as his English vocabulary increased along with his comfort level in his new environment, he began to act out in many ways. He verbally attacked his schoolmates, his sister, and even began to call us names. If Kent didn't like something we said, he would yell things like, "Shut up, stupid!" or, "Get away from me, poop-head [or worse]."

If we asked him to clean his room or put the dishes away and he was feeling out of sorts, he would scream, "No way, I hate you. Leave me alone!" When he didn't get his way with his sister or peers, he would sometimes throw something across the room to startle us. We tried several tactics to get him to stop this aggressive behavior, including time-outs and other logical consequences. Nothing was working very well until Emily called him "the gremlin" one day out of sheer frustration. This name took a playful twist and seemed to be just what the doctor ordered. Instead of continuing with our ineffective time-outs when he acted out, we began to interact with "the gremlin," as if he were a new character in our home.

When Kent would say something mean or rude, we would respond with, "Uh oh, the gremlin is back." We'd playfully warn the gremlin that we were going to "kiss him silly" if he didn't stop acting out. Soon it began to seem like more of a game than a problem. Adding the element of humor took some of the edge off and also let the gremlin know that he couldn't rile us up as much as he'd hoped.

Whenever we'd hear an off-color remark from Kent, we'd start talking to the gremlin, who could only communicate in groans, roars, and agonizing sounds, which we found very interesting. We might start to chase our son, and as we'd catch him, we'd pick him up, or he'd receive an onslaught of hugs or kisses from me or my husband, which the gremlin was "allergic to" but secretly seemed to enjoy. Sometimes we would wrestle in slow motion with him, which always made him laugh. And as soon as he laughed, the spell would be broken and the gremlin would disappear.

It was suggested to us by a child therapist that Kent's acting out was the only way he knew how to release some of his pent-up stress. Kent had gone from one poverty-stricken orphanage to another during the first few years of his life, and we suspected that he may have been subjected to some neglect, malnutrition, or abuse. A child psychologist friend suggested that we were doing groundbreaking work with our son by interacting with a disturbed and disruptive character that "wasn't the real Kent." All we knew was that it seemed to be working.

Within less than a year, the behavior problems were dramatically reduced. Kent took up theater at school and had a role in the school play. He gained a few new friends at school instead of ostracizing more kids. We reinforced the positive by acknowledging him for his politeness or good behavior whenever possible, and we continued to make light of his awkward character, the gremlin, who still slipped out from time to time.

As Kent became more trusting, the gremlin began to tell us morbid tales of "mean people, crying babies, and very hungry little children." When we'd offer to comfort the babies and children, he'd leap into one of our laps and turn into a baby himself. We'd wrap him in a big blanket, hold him close, bring him something to eat, and tell him that he was safe now. At this point, his underlying need for empathy and assurance had become more vulnerable and transparent, and we all considered it a victory.

Our son came up with many more interesting characters over the years to work through difficult emotions or to just make the family laugh! I encourage all parents to consider adding creativity, humor, and lightheartedness to make a very difficult situation manageable — and in the end, magical.

Use Natural Consequences Rather Than Punishment

The most precious of all possessions is power over ourselves.

— JOHN LOCKE

When children act out in ways that need correcting, there are two ways to handle the situation. The first is to punish the child, which conveys the message that their behavior is unacceptable or bad. The second is to implement a natural consequence, which lets a child know that there are consequences for his or her actions.

If a child tantalizes and teases his younger brother, for example, a random punishment might be a scolding, spanking, time-out, or deprivation of some sort (for example, no dessert or television that night). A natural consequence might be to request that he apologize in a sincere way to his brother and to talk out the problem, possibly with the help of an objective adult. The child may also be asked to help his brother in an activity of his brother's choice, such as teaching him to bat a ball — to make things right once again between him and his brother by offering constructive amends.

A teen getting poor grades in school might be grounded as a form of punishment. A natural consequence might include having the freedom to go out in direct proportion to how many hours are spent in study — every three hours of studying could earn one hour of going out. Here are a few of the major distinctions between the use of punishment and consequences:

The Use of Punishment

Objective: To discipline firmly with control or force; to command obedience

Message: Your behavior is bad or unacceptable; or you are bad or unacceptable

Approach: Serious, reactive, controlling, demanding, shaming, angry, or harsh

Characteristics: Inherently disrespectful while demanding respect; shaming, blaming, accusing, critical, or abusive; instills fear, resentment, or eventually apathy; often done in front of others for emphasis or effect; spanking, slapping, yelling, reprimanding, or punishing

Results: Temporarily stops behavior through fear, shame, or humiliation; the child is compliant out of fear, loses esteem, and may not be shown an appropriate alternative behavior; resistance, resentment, rebellion, withdrawal, or rage may develop over time; the child disconnects and distances from the adult in authority.

The Use of Natural Consequences

Objective: To correct with firm kindness; to teach accountability

Message: Your behavior needs improvement; you are still lovable

Approach: Responsive, direct, kind, firm, assuring, concerned, and consistent

Characteristics: Inherently respectful while requiring respect in return; encouraging, straightforward, affirming, and caring; instills values, responsibility, maturity,
and ownership; always done privately to honor all
involved; clear agreements, fair rules, accountability,
follow-through

Results: Transforms behavior by helping the child take
responsibility for any and all actions; the child feels
respected and learns to be cooperative; sensible ways
to make amends are learned; the child learns to trust
in oneself and in the world.

Respond Rather Than React

The disciplined one masters thoughts by stillness,
and emotions by calmness.

— LAO-TZU

The capacity to demonstrate grace under fire by responding
appropriately to a situation rather than overreacting is an art
and a skill. To respond is to *engage with presence.* To react is
to *act in opposition to.* Long-term resentment or estrangement
often occurs between a parent and child when a parent frequently flies off the handle in reaction or blows up unpre-
dictably over small grievances.

Adults can easily forget how frightening, stressful, or
even degrading it can be for a child to be randomly yelled at
or reprimanded for small mishaps that are part of growing up

and learning. All children need the security of knowing that the adults in their world are stable and able to handle the situations that arise with levelheadedness. The following story illustrates the powerful difference between reacting and responding to a crisis at hand:

Two young mothers, Carin and Stephanie, attended a county fair with their nine-year-old sons, Jason and Tyler, who were the best of friends. They were all having an exceptionally good time playing games, petting the prize-winning animals, and going on rides together. As lunchtime approached, the two mothers told the boys to wait for them near the Ferris wheel while they picked up some food.

In less than ten minutes, they returned with food in hand. Oddly enough, the boys were nowhere to be found. Since it wasn't a particularly busy day at the fair, it should have been easy to spot the boys. Carin immediately started to panic: "Jason would never just stray away on his own — he's been taught to not speak with strangers since he could talk," she said as she began to think the worst.

"Let's inform security," Stephanie said, as she tried to remain calm. Carin grabbed Stephanie's arm as her eyes welled up with tears. Stephanie made every effort to remain calm as she carefully described the boys to the security guards. After searching the entire park without success, panic sank in further, and the two worried mothers began to call other family members.

After another half hour of searching, each mother was growing increasingly stressed and concerned. Carin and Stephanie repeatedly called their sons' names throughout the fairgrounds. Suddenly, faint voices were heard from a distance. "Mom...Mom, over here. We're right here!" Carin and Stephanie were both shocked as they turned to see their boys walking toward them rather smugly and casually, as if nothing had happened.

Carin blurted out, "Where in God's name were you? We've been worried sick about the two of you!" "We snuck into the fun house through the back exit," Tyler said with a smirk. "We were hiding behind the mirrors and jumping out at people when they walked through. It was so cool! We scared this one lady so much she screamed! When we came out, the guard said you were looking for us. I guess we were in there longer than we thought."

The worried look on Carin's face was quickly replaced with a squinting scowl. "Is this true?" she asked as she turned to her son. "Answer me, Jason!" He nodded sheepishly and studied the pavement, avoiding eye contact. "You boys are a real nightmare!" Carin began to raise her voice. "You're never coming here again. We're going home so you can explain to your father exactly what you put us through today!"

Carin reached for her son, but he dodged her saying, "No way!" Carin was livid. She screamed, "Don't you talk to me like that! I'll slap you right here if you don't get over here now!" Jason ran away from his raging mother. "We should've lied and said we were almost kidnapped," he yelled as he ran. Carin replied with, "You'll wish you were kidnapped when we get home!" "I'm not going home. I don't have a home anymore," was Jason's last retort as he ran back into the park as fast as he could.

Stephanie and her son Tyler were a little dumbfounded as they took in the whole dramatic scene. Stephanie took a different approach with Tyler. "Can we talk for a minute, Ty?" "I guess," he responded with hesitation. "Tyler, we thought you guys were going to wait for us when we went to get food. Then we couldn't find you for so long, and we had no idea what happened to you. I'm upset that we were put through such a scare, and I'm surprised that the two of you would be so thoughtless about what we might be going through. On top of that, the prank you pulled was probably not the least bit funny to those who paid to have a good time. Who wants to be scared half to death by a couple of pranksters? Do you have anything to say about this?" she asked.

"Yeah," Tyler said, "I'm really sorry, Mom. We thought we'd go through the fun house one time. We were having so much fun, we had no idea how much time went by, and we kind of thought that the two of you would be talking and having fun like you usually are. I guess that was pretty dumb of us, huh."

Stephanie told Tyler she was glad he was okay and that it was important that he apologize to Carin and the security guards who all went through a needless scare. She told him to make sure he learned from this. He agreed and added that he now realized the importance of being more considerate. Because of the stress that his mother and Carin went through, they both agreed that a consequence of some sort was in order to make up for the scare and the lost time.

Tyler ended up apologizing to all concerned and then helped Carin to find Jason. As Carin observed the way Stephanie spoke to Tyler, and the way he responded, she began to realize she'd overreacted with her son. All four of them ended up having a long talk in the park as they shared their late lunch. Jason and Tyler were increasingly apologetic by the time they left the fairgrounds. Carin and Stephanie were increasingly understanding after talking more to the boys, realizing they had never intended to frighten or worry their mothers. What had been a crisis was transformed into a learning lesson, thanks to Stephanie's ability to respond rather than react in a difficult situation.

Exercises

1. Go Through the Twelve Signs Checklists

Take an inventory of your childhood home, followed by taking one of your home environment with your current family. How many of the old patterns are you repeating, and what new habits have you established? Circle the three greatest strengths from the list, and give yourself a pat on the back! Circle the three greatest weaknesses and make it an imperative to make the needed changes now.

2. The Respond-React Check-In

This week, check in to see if you are *responding* (engaging with presence), or *reacting* (acting in opposition) to situations that come up with your families. Take this exercise on with your kids, and exchange permission to tell one another if you are beginning to sweat over the small stuff or to create "mountains out of molehills." This is also a great exercise for couples to practice to shift draining or unnecessary arguments into productive discussions.

A MESSAGE FROM ALL CHILDREN ABOUT
DISCIPLINE WITH KINDNESS

Dear Parent or Guardian,
The ways you choose to discipline me
Bring dignity or shame to my world.

When you discipline me with anger,
You teach me to be rebellious.
When you discipline me with kindness,
You teach me to be humble.

When you correct me by punishing me,
You teach me to be defensive.
When you give me a natural consequence,
You teach me to be accountable.

So please correct me with kindness,
And treat me with respect.
I'll value you as my guardian
And grow into a responsible person.

CHAPTER SEVEN

Allow Room to Grow
and to Make Mistakes

Allow room for me to grow,
To make mistakes and have opinions.
I'll learn to be independent
And to trust my own judgment.

All human beings have at least two things in common: an infinite capacity to learn and an unlimited ability to make mistakes. As long as we are alive, human error will be part of our lives. Still, most of us experience some measure of shame, regret, or embarrassment when experiencing what we determine to be a "failure."

Irrational as it is to think we can go through life without making any small or big blunders, most of us are so wary of looking foolish or not getting things right that we avoid taking risks. The tragic result is living a halfhearted life, in which we laugh only part of our laughter, and cry only some of our tears. Equally tragic, our most cherished dreams may slip through our lives without ever getting a chance to blossom.

Mistakes Are Part of Learning

Mistakes are the portals of discovery.

— JAMES JOYCE

The three keys to moving successfully through mistakes are 1) to expect to make them, 2) to acknowledge them quickly, and 3) to ask the question, What can I learn from this? Every child needs the support of living in an environment where being less than perfect is perfectly acceptable, and even welcomed with open arms.

When a parent acknowledges a personal error, she models honesty and humility, and the effect on a child can only be positive. Children raised with adults who can say when they are wrong will learn to trust the world more and will admit to themselves and others when they have made a mistake.

Ted, a thirty-eight-year-old attorney, can still fondly recall how his father taught him the meaning of true humility when he was a teenager. He recalls a distressing time when his mother threatened his dad with a divorce if he didn't change his negative attitude, which was adversely affecting the whole family. His dad, renowned for complaining and bickering over even the smallest of things, was determined to shift this multigenerational pattern and break new ground to save his marriage and family. This was no easy task for him.

When he decided to repaint and remodel the garage and

guesthouse with the help of his two sons, he added a twist that took Ted and his brother by surprise. He agreed that if he began to complain, criticize, or get ornery, the work was done for the day and he'd owe his sons an hour of fun to make up for the unpleasant ordeal. Ted recalls with humor:

In the first few months, my dad had the capacity to work without criticizing or complaining for about half an hour at best. We played more football, catch, and miniature golf in the yard than we had in years! As soon as Dad came out with a put-down such as, "Gee-whiz, Ted, do you have to work so slow?" we'd call a time-out and go off to play — no excuses and no further questions asked by Dad.

Our mother could hardly believe her eyes when week after week she'd see us going off to the park with mitts and ball in hand. She never complained over the fact that the job was taking so long. She knew that the real renovation was taking place between Dad's two obstinate ears! We took as much pleasure witnessing our father fessing up to his relentless old habits as we did getting the extra playtime with him.

When the weather got cold and we were less than halfway done with the work, Dad became the butt of many family jokes. He was able to laugh right along with us, calling the half-painted garage and guesthouse his "anger-management project." The following spring we were back at it, and he was better, but far from 100 percent. As soon as his mood started to sour or he began to swear or complain, we could call a time-out and once again, we were free to toss the tools and play with Dad. This was especially annoying to him if it happened shortly after he'd mixed the paint, as it meant more backtracking. Still, he kept his end of the deal like a real trooper.

Dad actually reached the point where he could call a

time-out on himself after he'd blurt out an off-color comment or make a foul remark. He was really coming along. When we finally finished the job, it was time for a big celebration. We had a festive barbecue in the backyard with friends and neighbors, and my cousin's band played live music. Dad hadn't just remodeled our homestead; he'd remodeled his interior as well.

My dad successfully reduced his annoying habit of cursing under his breath by about 90 percent, and he changed from being a walking time bomb to a fairly cool and open-minded guy. Mom was elated and convinced he'd never have followed through without the help of his family. We all became skilled at painting that year, and even more important, we learned that overcoming old habits is possible — with a little bit of honesty, a lot of courage, and a few hundred time-outs and play breaks!

The Healing Power of an Apology

*Only those who dare to fail greatly
can ever achieve greatly.*

— JOHN F. KENNEDY

My mother, Diana, taught me much about apologizing through her own actions when I was a child. Her honesty is one reason that she is one of the people I most respect and admire in my life. If my mom found herself saying something unpleasant such as, "Your room is still such a mess, why isn't it cleaned up yet?" she'd often catch herself and say something like, "Oops...my old tape is playing again. I better play the new tape instead." Then she'd do something funny, like tap the side of her head as if shaking out the "old belief," which always got a chuckle out of me. Then she might start over again and say, "Could you please clean your room now? You'll feel so much better when it's clean."

On one occasion, she left me a note that said, "I'm sorry for all of the ways I might have hurt you that I don't even realize." I think she wrote it after reading one of her favorite Socrates quotes: "There is only one thing I know for certain, and that is that I know very little." She often included empathy when apologizing. She might say, "I'm sorry you had to wait so long at the store. It must have been frustrating for you." I was free to respond with, "It was a really long time, Mom, and you said we'd only be there for half an hour!" She'd often find a way to make up for it by spending extra time with me or by taking me to the park. It's pretty hard to stay upset with someone who can admit a mistake and see the other person's point of view too. The following simple steps will help children and parents to make effective amends:

Four Steps to Making Amends

1. *Tell the truth.* Be honest about what happened and make a sincere apology.

2. *Show empathy.* Be understanding of the other person's point of view.

3. *Listen.* Hear the other person's response and concerns without defense.

4. *Take action.* Show in deed and not just in words that you are sincere in your efforts.

A Spoonful of Humor Helps
the Humility Go Down

*The only man who never makes a mistake
is the man who never does anything.*

— THEODORE ROOSEVELT

Since we all make mistakes, using humor to put things in perspective is a wonderful and economical way to save hours of stress lamenting over foibles and mishaps that, in the long run, just aren't all that important.

My grandparents had a wonderful way of making light of their mistakes. Their sense of humor was evident and undoubtedly contributed to their marriage of more than fifty years. My grandfather would sometimes fall into an ornery spell in the late afternoons before dinner. My grandmother would joke about it and say it was age reversal — he'd been cranky as a baby, and he was getting cranky again now that he was growing old.

Grandpa would bicker and complain over a gadget that needed fixing or begin to talk to Grandma with an edge in his voice. Instead of letting the tension escalate into an argument, Grandma would diffuse it by saying, "Look who's back — it's the old goat," while cracking a little smile. At that point, the grandchildren would come running into the room in anticipation of what often came next. Grandpa would respond by bellowing out the longest, shrillest goat sound we'd ever heard! Then, to be extra funny, he might strut around like a goat, or let out a few more of his unbelievably loud goat sounds. By then the grandkids would be heaped in a pile on the couch and in stitches, laughing as though we'd never heard these things before.

Their infamous "old goat" routine was Grandma's clever way of calling Grandpa on his moodiness in a lighthearted way. Grandpa's entertaining response was his way of admitting his weakness in good fun. They taught us well that a little bit of humor definitely does help the humility go down.

Offer Support in Times of Difficulty

To be there in good times is human;
to be there in bad times is divine.

— MOTHER TERESA

When a person makes a poor choice, it can be grueling to take the consequences of the actions. The Persian mystic Jelaluddin Rumi referred to this process as "sitting in the fire." In times like these, having caring, nonjudgmental support to lean on is a real godsend. The following story illustrates the value of a father's loving support in his daughter's time of need.

Rose, a young woman of twenty-two, recounts a time when her father played a profound role in my life as she was about to make "one of the biggest mistakes of my life," as she put it. She was engaged to her high school sweetheart, despite the concerns of her friends, who didn't particularly like him. Everything in her life seemed to be moving along wonderfully, until her whole world changed overnight.

To her shock and surprise, Rose was informed of her fiancé's ongoing infidelity with one of her friends just weeks before the wedding. In a panic, she decided that she'd go through with getting married regardless. She loved this man and desperately wanted to believe that the life they'd planned together would surely heal him of this weakness. But her body and emotions seemed to know otherwise. Despite her insistence that "everything was going to be okay," she fell into a deep depression and still hadn't come out of it one week before the wedding.

Nothing seemed to console her as she lay listlessly in her old bedroom at her parents' house. It was then that her father, Hal, realized he needed to come to the aid of his youngest daughter in her time of need. He was by no means versed in communication, and he didn't have the faintest idea how to talk to his daughter about such a personal, uncomfortable matter. Still, he knew that he must do something to support Rose without seeming pushy or invasive.

Hal took the entire day off and made it his personal mission to support his daughter in making a good choice and coming out of her depression. In the morning, he brought Rose her favorite magazine on a tray, along with a delicious breakfast. He knocked in a silly rhythm on the bedroom door and said, "Open the door, sleepyhead, there's an important delivery here. I'll just leave it by the door."

When she didn't respond, he put a CD player near the door and played a well-loved song she'd played repeatedly in high school, which he often asked her to turn down. When the door finally opened, Rose peeked out to discover the pleasant offerings and cracked a faint smile. "Thanks, Dad, but I'm not very hungry," she said. He had a toolbox ready in hand and cheerfully asked if he could get into the room for just a moment to check the heater. Reluctantly, she let him into the room to have a look at the vent (which happened to be working just fine, as Hal already knew).

While examining the heater, he attempted a few minutes of small talk. He let her know he had the day off if she needed anything. When his efforts at reaching her didn't work, he stepped out on a limb and blurted out unrehearsed, "Honey, it makes me so sad to see you going through all this. I wish I could protect you from the world sometimes and take away your pain. I just want you to know I'm here for you in any way you need me."

His words caught her off guard. She burst into tears as he sat down beside her and put his arm around her. For a time, he just listened as she poured her tears and heartache out. He'd never had a moment with her like this before. He wasn't sure how to respond, so at first he didn't say anything at all. He just listened with intermittent sighs and nods, asking her an occasional question to show that he cared about her thoughts and feelings.

Rose had the energy to get out of bed by midmorning and even helped her dad later on with yard work as they continued to talk. She couldn't seem to get enough of his attention and listening ear. Eventually, as his daughter became quiet, Hal told her of an early heartbreak of his own, before his marriage to Rose's mother. He shared more about his life, telling her things she'd never known. Rose learned how he'd started a successful business only after the huge disappointment of being fired from a job he thought he'd have forever. For a simple man of few words, Rose's dad had some real wisdom to share with her.

By the following day, Rose gained a new sense of clarity and told her fiancé the relationship was over. With the support of her family and friends, she steered herself in a whole new direction and enrolled in college the next semester. A few years later, when she was graduating with honors, she added the following to her short graduating speech: "I think it was the love of my father, who was there for me during my lowest low, that helped lead me to this moment of victory. Thanks, and I love you, Dad, from the very bottom of my heart."

The Steep Price of Perfectionism

Perfectionism is a disease of the mind, for the heart knows that life is far too fleeting to be taken too seriously.

— ANTOINE DE SAINT-EXUPÉRY

Children who are raised in austere homes are more likely to take their problems seriously and feel ashamed of making mistakes. Children who are not encouraged or taught to be forgiving of themselves or others may find life reduced to a series of obstacles to overcome. Since most of us were not raised with role models who take their mistakes in stride and learn from them, there is an epidemic of adults who make excuses, blame others, or cover up their errors to save face.

Joanie, a forty-six-year-old mother of two children, recalls growing up with a caring but relentless father who seemed to make it a way of life to point out her mistakes rather than offering recognition for what she did well. She recalls a defining moment in high school that has stayed with her to this day. One semester, Joanie worked especially hard on all her subjects and made the honor roll with seven A's and one B. Confident that her father would be thrilled with her progress, she couldn't wait to show him her report card and to see his glowing face when he saw that she had a close-to-perfect report card!

When she arrived home and saw her father seated at his desk, she rushed into the den and proudly handed her report card to him. He carefully examined it for what seemed like

an eternity, and then said, "Seven A's and one B. Hmm...
what did you get the B in?" That was it — the full extent of
his comments. There was no acknowledgment, congratula-
tions, or celebration — just Joanie's dad singling out the one
less-than-perfect score. She was devastated and left the room
in tears. The next semester, her grades plummeted to three
B's and four C's. The following year, her grades were even
lower. To this day, she monitors her tendency to zero in on
her mistakes and to overlook her successes.

Over the years, Joanie has had a number of talks with her
kids about this, determined to allow room for them to be
imperfect. To help instill this lesson, a few times a year they
have a "marvelous mistakes meal." Each of them shares a few
of the mistakes they've made recently and what can be
learned from each. "It's a real eye opener, and the kids love it
— especially when it's my turn! Our latest aspiration is to
have my father over some time for a marvelous mistakes
meal. We know it's a risk, but the worst thing that could happen is that it blows up in our face, which would make a great
topic at our next dinner!"

Find the Good in the Mistake

*What is a weed? A plant whose virtues
have not yet been discovered.*

— RALPH WALDO EMERSON

I was recently in a grocery store checkout line with a bustling
sense of hurry and impatience in the air. A busy mother and
her preschool-aged son stood directly in front of me. I
watched as the child entertained himself while his mother

slowly moved her cart through the line. The boy was pushing a toy truck along the floor and singing to himself gleefully. As the two approached the register, he accidentally bumped into a large candy container. Little foil-wrapped candies went rolling all over the floor between the shoppers and their carts.

I was right behind them when it happened, so I smiled and said, "Oops!" as I helped pick up the little candies beneath my feet. As the woman realized what her son had done, her face turned red with embarrassment. This was just a minor incident in my mind, so her reaction really surprised me. She yanked her son by the arm and shook him harshly while she spat out the words, "You are a naughty, naughty boy!" She gritted her teeth and threatened him in a mean tone of voice, "You're going to get a good, hard spanking when we leave this store." The little boy began to whimper as he tried to wrench free of his mother's tightening grip. The woman rolled her eyes as she glanced over at me, hoping to gain my sympathy. I was bothered by her overreaction and couldn't help but empathize with her young son, who now feared getting a spanking as soon as they reached the parking lot.

I'm not an advocate of spanking and believe that good communication has a much better effect on a child. I avoided eye contact with the woman and felt myself holding back my urge to tell her off for the way she treated her son. I wanted to yell at her the same way she'd just yelled at her boy and say, "How can you put him to shame for something that was just an accident, and why would you want to spank a small child? What's wrong with you? Are you from the dark ages? Can't you see that you're damaging him, not disciplining him?"

I let this flood of emotion pass and refrained from voicing my opinion. I knew my gut reaction was no better than hers, and that it would have a poor effect if I made a scene. I realized it wasn't the time or place to fight for the rights of children by making an example out of her. I took a moment to calm down and just breathe. And then I took an opportunity to do something entirely different.

Rather than insulting her or making her look bad, I decided to compliment her frightened little boy. "Your son is just adorable," I said with a smile. She seemed surprised to hear this and mumbled something about his being naughty. The child stopped and stared at me incredulously. I continued with, "I was noticing the creative way he can keep himself occupied. He has quite an imagination!" She smiled sheepishly and said that he probably got that from his father, who was a cartoon animator. I marveled over his precocious intelligence when she told me he was only three years old.

The young boy was keenly aware of the shift in his mother's tone of voice as she told me about his achievements in day care, his beautiful artwork, and how he already knew how to use the computer. "Wow," I exclaimed as I turned to look the sweet little boy in the eyes. "You're a very special person. I'll bet there's no one like you in the whole wide world!" To my surprise, the little boy leaped toward me and flung his arms around my legs. "Oh, my goodness, and you give the best hugs too," I said as his mother and I laughed together.

The mood had shifted entirely in just a few short minutes once I found the good in her son and acknowledged it. As the two of them were leaving the store, I could see the glimmer return to the child's eyes as his mom affectionately told him to say good-bye to me. He waved both hands happily as I blew him a kiss. When I reached the parking lot a few minutes later, I heard sounds of laughter. I looked off in the distance to see the woman tickling her young son as she helped him into the car.

In a small but significant way, I knew I'd gifted the little boy by helping his mother to see how precious he was, despite the minor mishap. They probably had a better night because of it, and one precious little child was spared a needless punishment and appreciated just a little bit more.

Encourage Independent Thinking

Small is the number of them that see with their own eyes and feel with their own hearts.

— ALBERT EINSTIEN

In a world where many people are denied their basic human rights, most Americans value freedom even more than ever before. We have freedom of speech, freedom of worship, and the freedom to pursue our values and interests on many levels. But how many of us grew up in democratic households where we were free to think and live outside our family's perceptions, values, and judgments?

I once asked a lecture hall of more than two thousand educators how many of them had been encouraged to think for themselves and to have an opinion outside their families as they were growing up. I was met with dumbfounded looks and blank stares. A handful of people raised their hands, while the majority pondered my next question: How is it that so few family systems make room for perspectives other than their own, especially those of their children? How does this affect their rapport — and the world, for that matter?

One woman raised her hand and surprised the entire room by describing an activity that her father had brought to the family. Every month, they had a family debate, choosing a hot topic that was current in the news. Each family member would bring a different perspective to the discussion to prevent "the keyhole syndrome," which her father claimed would develop if "one's perspective became so narrow that you could look through a keyhole with both eyes at the same time!"

Sometimes they discussed a political candidate running for office; other times they debated national issues such as capital punishment, abortion, or terrorism. Since her father highly encouraged his children to explore perspectives other than their own, their debates were a stimulating way to expand their thinking. The children were encouraged to hold their assigned point of view, even if it was not their own. This meant reading up on the issue from the angle they would be representing. Because of this game, this woman and her siblings became familiar with newspapers and publications, both traditional and alternative, as she was growing up.

One of the family debate rules was that all perspectives were to be honored as having equal value. They were encouraged by their father to listen to all sides of an issue with respect before forming an opinion. This is quite a radical departure from the political debates that take place in the United States prior to elections, where opponents bait, challenge, and sometimes denigrate one another in the name of fair politics. The entire auditorium wanted to know if her family still conducted the debates now that she and her siblings were grown up. "We don't have to feign a monthly debate anymore now that we're grown," she said with a smile. "We're all so different in perspective by nature, thanks to my father, that every time we get together, we have lively debates and dialogues on many, many topics!"

I was inspired by her story and wished I'd had the opportunity to meet her father in person. He was way ahead of his time encouraging his children to think for themselves instead of becoming cultural lemmings. It is rare to find a person at any age who truly thinks for him- or herself. Einstein believed that most people "don't really think; they simply rearrange their prejudices." Mahatma Gandhi was once asked what he thought of Western civilization. His reply was, "I think it's a good idea."

Exercises

1. Practice the Four Steps to Making Amends

Few things are as appreciated as a sincere apology. Since we all unwittingly hurt or offend one another on occasion, make it a practice to go through all four steps when saying you're sorry. Encourage your children to do the same with family members, and especially with their peers and elders. The rapport and rewards are well worth every ounce of effort.

2. Have a "Marvelous Mistakes Meal"

Schedule a "marvelous mistakes meal" in the near future with a few trusted friends or family members, and celebrate the lessons you have learned from a few of your recent blunders. Bring a few current challenges to the table, and brainstorm together on the ways that you can find the gift in the error and the good in the mistake.

~

A MESSAGE FROM ALL CHILDREN ABOUT
ALLOWING ROOM TO GROW

Dear Parent or Guardian,
Your attitude about making mistakes
Will influence my well-being
For better or worse.

When you reprimand me,
You teach me to avoid taking risks.
When you make light of my error,
You teach me to try and try again.

When you shame me for my opinions,
You teach me to keep to myself.
When you encourage me to think for myself,
You teach me to be independent.

So please allow room for me to grow,
To make mistakes and think for myself.
I'll learn to trust my judgment
And grow to make good choices.

CHAPTER EIGHT

Model Lifelong Learning

Stay interested in learning
And following your dreams.
I'll pick up your enthusiasm
And be inspired to do the same.

Learning is a lifelong pursuit that begins even before we leave the womb and continues until we die. Learning allows us to progress and improve and to gain valuable knowledge and wisdom. It strengthens us and enriches our lives while presenting us with new possibilities. For these reasons and more, instilling a love of learning at an early age will give a child a lifelong advantage.

Reading books and stories aloud, playing games and puzzles, doing projects together, hiking, exploring nature, caring for living things, taking classes of all kinds, sharing hobbies and the arts, watching movies and documentaries, playing sports, singing, dancing, cultural events, travel, being of service, and sharing the inestimable tasks and lessons of daily life are just a few of the ways we can facilitate ongoing learning experiences that enrich our children.

Come Alive with Learning!

Ask not what the world needs. Ask what makes you come alive... then go do it. Because what the world most needs is people who have come alive.

— HOWARD THURMAN

An equally influential and often overlooked way to instill a lifelong desire to learn in our children is to be passionately involved in learning ourselves. Few things are more exciting for children than being near an enthusiastic grown-up who is on fire with the pursuit of learning. Unfortunately, many adults lose sight of their natural curiosities and passions over the years, leading lukewarm lifestyles in which "settling" is the norm.

The late Leo Buscaglia, inspirational author and speaker extraordinaire, had a talent for rousing the public as few orators have been able to do. He attributed much of his vociferous gusto to his father. To Leo's father, life was one great learning quest, and he wished to instill the same fervor in his own children. One of the questions he asked each of his children daily was, "What did you learn today?" Leo's dad insisted that his children come to the dinner table each night with something interesting to share. He participated as well, sharing various life lessons or perspectives on any number of subjects. Leo and his siblings would bring tidbits from school subjects and anything else they could think of. On many occasions, Leo had to scurry off to the encyclopedia shortly before dinner and come up with an attention-grabbing or obscure fact that he could share with the family.

His father's eyes would widen with wonder as each of his children shared his or her contribution. Whenever he heard something he didn't know, he would sigh deeply, clasp his chin, and say, "That is fascinating. Did anyone here know that?" Only much later in life did Leo realize how stimulating this nightly activity had been. Throughout his life, no matter how late it was when he retired for the night, he would ask himself, "Leo, what did you learn today?" He couldn't rest or go to sleep until he had an answer to his own inquiry.

Forty-year-old Karan fondly recalls all that he learned from his dearly loved grandmother, Pema, who moved to the United States to join him and his family when she was seventy-five. In her home country of Iran, she didn't need to know how to drive a car since she lived in a small village and usually traveled by foot. Living in Los Angeles, she quickly learned, was a whole different story. For the first few years, Pema was dependent on relatives, taxis, and buses to get from one place to another. Over time, as she became more famil-iar with the country and the English language, Pema was determined to drive on her own, even though the family was concerned that she was "too old."

Despite their protests, Pema went ahead and signed up for her first driver's education class at the age of seventy-eight. Most of her classmates were younger than her grand-children. It took her three attempts to pass the written test, and a few more than that to pass the driving test. When Pema finally earned a valid driver's license, she was as elated as a child at a birthday party, and she even baked a cake to celebrate!

The mobility that a driver's license granted Pema allowed her to attend a local community college at the age of eighty. She eventually earned a two-year degree in community education, receiving special merit for being the oldest person ever to complete the program. She put her training to good use by offering senior enrichment courses at a local retirement home, which she continued to do with great enthusiasm until her passing at the age of ninety-two.

"Those last twelve years were some of the best years of her life," Karan reflects, "because she wasn't really getting older, just better. She'd been a wife and mother all her life in Iran, raising five children, seven grandchildren, and four great-grandchildren. She was very proud of her family, but she always dreamed of traveling to the United States. Well, she not only traveled here, she lived here, learned the language, got a driver's license, earned an associate degree, and became a teacher — and a well-loved one at that." Karan attributes much of his ambition and persistence to his grandmother Pema, who demonstrated so much savoir faire throughout her life.

Learn New Things Together as a Family

I am still learning.

— MICHELANGELO

When my mom, Diana, and I decided that we wanted to get a puppy when I was a teen, we had no idea what we were in for. We imagined nurturing and playing with a cuddly little creature, but it wasn't until we brought our four-legged little friend home that we discovered the enormous amount of work that having a puppy entails. Between the constant need for attention, the messy accidents on the carpet, the shoe wrecking, the chair gnawing, the holes in the lawn, and the separation anxiety that our little dog had whenever we left his sight, it was a bit overwhelming. Our first weeks with Toby, our new little pug, were like having a baby in the house twenty-four hours a day plus.

When training him proved to be more challenging than we'd thought it would be, we realized it was time to take our precious pet to doggie-training classes. Since we shared the responsibilities of taking care of Toby, it was important for both of us to go to the classes so that we'd train him using the same techniques. This proved to be effective and a ton of fun!

The class was taught by a cheerful couple with an extended family of six canines, all attending class as shining examples of proper doggie etiquette. The dogs were attentive, intelligent, and well behaved and seemed to instinctively know that the unruly young pups were undergoing training. They displayed incredible patience and barked loudly if one of the puppies wandered away from the training area. We had hours of enjoyment as we showed Toby just how far his training could take him in his pursuit of human approval. After each class, my mom and I would chuckle for days, recalling our pudgy little pug plodding through his lessons in puppy politeness. Toby was considered the show-off and jester of the class, always seeking the accolades and attention from the onlookers.

What a pleasure it was for my mom and me to be acquiring the knowledge needed to raise an angelic (well, almost) pooch while sharing a new learning experience together. We acquired great dog-training skills from the very best trainers while having a great time.

It wasn't long before Toby became quite a charmer. By the time the course was over, we had a class-act little tail-wagger in the house who could wait until invited to be petted when company arrived and stay in the next room when we ate dinner rather than begging for scraps under the table. Toby could even sit perfectly still while I'd dress him in my old baby clothes and pose him for a picture (with the anticipated reward of his favorite bacon treats, of course). After successfully completing the dog-training class, we decided to take horseback riding lessons at a local ranch together, which was equally enjoyable. Our shared animal ventures have been a lot of fun and have brought us many warmhearted memories.

Joel, an eighteen-year-old high school senior, recalls the fun he had during his fifteenth summer when his mother, Erin, decided to enroll in skateboarding classes with him. It started out as a joke — he didn't have his driver's license yet and was dependent on his mother for transportation to the class. Since the drive was a distance each way, Erin told her son, "Heck, Joel, for all that driving, I might as well take the class with you!"

After thinking it over, Joel's mom decided to do just that. She did have good coordination and had been an excellent roller skater in high school. Besides, it could be a great aerobic workout. At first Joel was mortified and insisted that they walk in separately so his classmates wouldn't know that the "older woman" in class was related to him. Since Joel's mom had an easygoing personality and was not half-bad at skateboarding, she was well received by the class. Eventually, the group found out that Erin was Joel's mother. They responded with comments like "Your mom is cool" and "My mother would never try something like this."

At the end of the eight weeks, Joel and Erin both had a

few skateboarding tricks to proudly show off to their family. Even though Joel's mom didn't continue to pursue skateboarding, she did practice her newfound skills in the long driveway or at the nearby park. Taking the class made her feel younger and more upbeat. Erin gained the impetus to sign up for classes she'd been too fearful to try before, including tango lessons and stock investing. Erin and Joel both benefited greatly from the shared learning experience. Joel got to see his mother trying something new and different, and Erin felt rejuvenated after doing something she didn't think she could do.

Learn about the Seven Areas of Intelligence

Everyone is born a genius.
But the process of life de-geniuses you.

— BUCKMINSTER FULLER

One of the most limiting practices in the field of education has been the use of the term gifted to single out a few over the many. Every person is *gifted* in his or her own way — it's just a matter of discovering personal talents and developing them. Howard Gardner, a Harvard psychology professor, has identified at least seven "intelligence centers" in the human brain. His research, which has been well received, expands our narrow perceptions of intelligence to include a number of areas that have not been previously acknowledged.

Becoming aware of the seven areas of intelligence is an excellent start in identifying each family member's areas of greatest talent and interest. While certain cultures and societies place higher value on one or more of the intelligence centers, these areas are all equally valuable in contributing to one's learning enrichment.

The Seven Areas of Intelligence

1. _____ *Bodily kinesthetic intelligence.* Bodily kinesthetic intelligence is well developed in those interested in sports, bodybuilding, marathons, stunts, mechanical skills, handicrafts, or any activity that involves physical challenge. Those high in bodily kinesthetic intelligence have highly developed responsiveness to the physical environment. They are agile and athletic, with exceptional body control. They have excellent coordination, good reflexes, and keen mechanical and crafting skills.

2. _____ *Visual-spatial intelligence.* Visual-spatial intelligence is most often seen in those interested in visual arts, maps, charts, diagrams, and the use of metaphor. Drawing, painting, jewelry making, architecture, interior design, sculpting, and mapmaking are just a few professions of interest. Those with visual-spatial interest have an eye for color and beauty and a knack for decorating and design. They are keenly aware of form, dimension, and space.

3. _____ *Linguistic intelligence.* Linguistic intelligence is observed in those who love to read, write, and listen. They have a passion for the spoken and written word and usually excel in spelling, writing, storytelling, editing, and pronunciation. They have a good memory for trivia and are

clever with one-liners. Those with linguistic intelligence have a vast vocabulary and often speak several languages. They like crossword puzzles and word games, and often win spelling bees or debates. They may be good spokespeople, or they may prefer written communication.

4. _____ *Logical-mathematical intelligence.* Logical-mathematical intelligence is strongly developed in those who are adept in science, math, engineering, law, and accounting, to name a few disciplines. People with this kind of intelligence like numbers, problem solving, investigating, logical experimentation, processing, and abstract thinking. They have a special affinity with computers, calculators, and technical gadgets of all sorts.

5. _____ *Musical intelligence.* Those with musical intelligence are attuned to rhythm, pitch, beat, timbre, and sound of all kinds. They love complex musical arrangements and the emotional power of music. People who are endowed with musical intelligence enjoy creating and listening to music of all kinds. They might be composers, music teachers, singers, symphony conductors, voice-over artists, recording engineers, performers, or producers.

6. _____ *Interpersonal intelligence.* Interpersonal intelligence is well developed in "people people," including teachers, politicians, salespeople, public speakers, leaders, and personal relations

professionals. They usually have lots of friends
and colleagues, communicate and negotiate
well, like to work on group projects, and tend
to be involved in a number of groups and
associations. They enjoy taking on leadership
roles and highly value influencing others.

7. _____ *Intrapersonal intelligence.* Intrapersonal intelligence
is commonly found among philosophers,
counselors, poets, mystics, wise elders, religious
leaders, and spiritual mentors. Those with
intrapersonal intelligence are tuned in to their
life purpose and sensitive to the feelings, needs,
and aspirations of others. They are relatively
unaffected by mainstream thinking and bring
timeless wisdom and soulful perspective to all
that they do. They aspire to serve and help others
and invoke transformation and positive change.

An individual may be highly developed in one or more
areas, and weak in the others. A person may be somewhat
balanced in all areas, or she may exhibit any combination. In
different stages of life, an individual may favor one or more
of the areas. A teenaged boy might put most of his interest in
bodily kinesthetic intelligence if he is athletic and sports
driven. As he matures and goes to college, he may discover a
propensity for law and writing, developing new interest in
logical-mathematical intelligence and linguistic intelligence.

Rate yourself and family in the seven intelligence areas in
two ways. First, rate your natural talents in each of the intelligence areas from 1 to 7, with the area in which you have the
most talent being 1 and the one in which you have the least
talent being 7.

Go over the seven areas of intelligence a second time, and rate your interest level (with 1 being of little or no interest and 5 being of strong interest). If you feel you have minimal talent in the area of musical intelligence but have great interest in learning to play the piano, then rate it a 5. If you are highly capable in the area of mathematical intelligence but have very little interest in pursuing the area further, rate it as a 1 or 2.

After rating your natural talents and interest levels, choose an intelligence area that rates high in both areas, and consider making it the next intelligence area to develop more. To gain even greater perspective, ask a family member or trusted friend to rate your natural talents and interest levels and see how your scores match.

The Twelve Tools of Intelligence

Intelligence is one of the greatest gifts
and mysteries of all time.

— CARL SAGAN

Understanding intelligence is a very recent development in our evolution. We are still in the infancy stages of understanding what we are capable of. Some years ago, while teaching at a university, I taught a course in brain research and intelligence. With the help and feedback of my students, I compiled a list of fundamental tools of intelligence. These twelve tools are part of the intelligence repertoire of every normal individual. To the degree that we've developed each of these tools, we're able to effectively use more of our intelligence to succeed and move forward in life. Read through the following to consider your current aptitudes:

The Twelve Tools of Intelligence

1. _____ *Adaptability:* The capacity to adapt and adjust to new situations well

2. _____ *Concentration:* The capacity to focus and filter out distractions

3. _____ *Creativity:* The capacity to think in new and different ways and to envision what is not yet in existence

4. _____ *Discernment:* The capacity to distinguish one thing from another — the good from the bad, the false from the true, the helpful from the harmful

5. _____ *Editing:* The capacity to edit out negativity, prejudice, projection, and irrelevant or outdated information from one's thoughts or environment

6. _____ *Emotional literacy:* The capacity to understand the feelings and needs of oneself and others and to act empathically and appropriately

7. _____ *Feedback:* The capacity to actively seek and receive feedback and to alter one's behavior in order to be more effective

8. _____ *Possession of knowledge:* The capacity to draw from a diversified and well-rounded base of knowledge

9. _____ *Memory:* The capacity to recall and play back information and events with accuracy

10. _____ *Processing:* The capacity to comprehend and interpret information correctly without the filters of prejudice or preconception

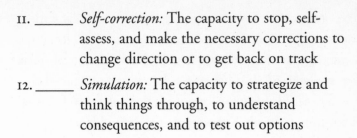

11. _____ *Self-correction:* The capacity to stop, self-assess, and make the necessary corrections to change direction or to get back on track

12. _____ *Simulation:* The capacity to strategize and think things through, to understand consequences, and to test out options

Rate yourself and your children (over the age of twelve) in each of the twelve areas from 1 to 5, with 1 being little aptitude developed and 5 being a high degree of aptitude developed. Choose one of the tools with a low rating, and make it an aim to raise your score by creating an action plan.

An elderly woman scored herself highest in adaptability and possession of knowledge, having lived in many parts of the world as an international negotiator. Her lowest rating was in editing and self-correction, since she was set in her ways and had been repeating several poor habits for many years. Her action plan was to consult a mentor to help her change a few of her most stubborn habits (such as smoking, drinking too much coffee, and sleeping in late) and to enlist the help of her best friend to hold her accountable in a short daily phone call.

A middle-aged screenwriter found that he was strongest in creativity because of his work. However, he was weakest in simulation because he tended to make impulsive decisions. His action plan was to write out a pros and cons list and to create a list of smart questions to answer before making a big decision. He also decided to check in with a trusted friend or mentor when necessary.

A young woman in high school found that she was strongest in emotional literacy, since she had been trained as a teen mediator and was naturally empathetic with others. Her weakest area was concentration, since she had difficulty settling down to get her homework done or to plan her day. Her action plan was to take a few minutes to get still and completely relax before studying to clear her mind. It was recommended that she set a timer for forty-five-minute periods of study, followed by a ten-minute break. Knowing that she could have frequent breaks would help her to concentrate more.

Learn from Some of the Great Late Bloomers

Obstacles cannot crush me. Every obstacle yields to stern resolve. He who is fixed to a star does not change his mind.

— LEONARDO DA VINCI

Some of the most famous and revered people throughout history have been unique in their learning styles and did not necessarily conform to the norm. Their special gifts were often not recognized by their contemporaries because they didn't follow the beaten path. More often than not, they blazed a trail that had not existed before.

To help children overcome challenges, learn more about the lives of some the greatest thinkers who were able to move through their challenges and break new ground. Here is a list of just a few of the most brilliant and misunderstood learners of all time:

- Ludwig van Beethoven had a music teacher who was convinced he didn't have any talent at all and said, "As a composer, he is hopeless."

- Thomas Edison was told as a boy that he was too stupid to learn anything.

- Helen Keller was born with the double challenge of being blind and deaf and became one of the most inspirational philosophers and writers of her time.

- Gustave Flaubert found it extremely difficult to read as a child.

- Isaac Newton scored the lowest academically in his grade school class.

- Enrico Caruso was told by a music teacher, "You have no voice at all."

- Walt Disney was fired when he worked as a newspaper editor because "he didn't have any good ideas."

- Winston Churchill failed the sixth grade.

- Rosa Parks, an unknown African American seamstress, refused to get off a bus and sparked the civil rights movement.

- Thomas Aquinas was dubbed the "dumb ox" at school.

- Johann Pestalozzi, a foremost Swiss educator, was regarded as wild and foolish by school authorities.

- Leo Tolstoy flunked out of college.

- Virginia Woolf, who suffered from bipolar disorder, became one of the greatest writers of the twentieth century.

- Albert Einstein was four years old before he could speak, and seven before he could read. One of his grade school teachers said, "He'll never make a success of anything" and recommended that he take up a trade.

- The Duke of Wellington failed in many of his classes throughout school.

- Louisa May Alcott was told by an editor that she could never write anything with popular appeal.

- Louis Pasteur was rated mediocre in college chemistry.

- Abraham Lincoln entered the Black Hawk War as a captain and was demoted to a private when he came out.

Virtually everyone has difficulty at some time in his or her life. Children need to understand that it isn't how many times one fails that determines success or failure; it is how many times one gets up and tries again that determines the final outcome. Imagine if the great people above had taken their failures or critics too seriously. They might have given up and simply stopped trying. The tragic result would have been that the world would have been deprived of their invaluable contributions.

Winston Churchill put it well in a renowned speech he gave to a graduating class of seniors at a prestigious English institution. He looked around the room for a full ten minutes before saying, "Never give up" in a thunderously loud voice. Then he paused for a long time as he looked each graduating senior in the eye before speaking again. After drawing in a deep breath, he reiterated, "Never give up" with an even greater sense of urgency and command in his voice.

After a third interval of long, deafening silence, he shouted out, "Never give up" with vigor and force, and then he simply walked off the stage. Needless to say, it was a memorable speech — and certainly one that no one in attendance would ever forget. He received one of the longest standing ovations in the history of public speaking.

It's Never Too Late to Follow Your Dreams

*I would rather be ashes than dust. I would rather
that my spark should burn out in a brilliant blaze
than it should be stifled by dry rot.*

— JACK LONDON

When I was seven my father, Lou, was compelled to embark on one of the biggest adventures of his life, showing me that unwavering persistence can make a dream come true. In his thirties he decided to boldly step out of his established carpentry business and pursue his lifelong dream of becoming a doctor.

My dad was a hardworking, down-to-earth guy with nose-to-the-grindstone work ethics. He came from a small farming community in Wisconsin, and most of his relatives were farmers. It was a big stretch for a country boy in his thirties to be envisioning such a lofty and far-reaching goal, and he wasn't exactly encouraged. Many thought him foolish to be letting go of the one thing that held a roof over our heads to chase what seemed like a young man's fantasy. It certainly was a stretch, but my dad believed he could reach his goal with enough hard work and persistence.

After he painstakingly completed the needed undergraduate courses and applied at a well-respected medical college, we all held our breath and waited. I'll never forget the day my dad walked through the door with a letter in hand from the Medical College of Wisconsin. This was the letter that would determine his fate, either accepting him as one of the chosen few out of hundreds of applicants or politely refusing his admission, forcing him to fall back on his previous work.

With trembling hands, he opened the letter and read

aloud his acceptance, to his own amazement. He was elated, and we were all overjoyed for him. In the middle of his already full life, my father soon took the plunge headfirst into medical school. His years of studying the wonders of medicine were grueling, and I witnessed my dad's pursuit with fascination and admiration. I spent a number of my growing years doing homework side by side with him. He'd spend hours upon days upon weeks upon months getting through thick books about infectious diseases and their antidotes. The intense exams he studied for would have floored the average college student, and many nights he was up late with coffee in hand, preparing for the next gargantuan exam.

The fact that my dad was older than the rest of his classmates by almost fifteen years didn't deter him one bit. He was well liked by other students because he was friendly and had a unique flair. Most of his classmates didn't have any responsibilities to juggle and hadn't experienced the diversity of life that he had. His professors favored him for his studious determination.

For a time, I watched my father study like a madman most afternoons and evenings, and then work a third-shift job starting at 3 A.M. just to scrape by, while stretching school loans as far as he could. He even built a few extra rooms in his basement so that he could take in a couple of roommates. Money was tight, but he was tenacious, and the final outcome always seemed to outweigh the struggle.

I recall the wildly creative measures my dad took to sustain his drive during those unending hours. One of his more adventurous endeavors involved building a suspended study loft in a corner of the living room. He suspended a few large wooden slabs using thick chains to hang them from the ceiling.

They lay horizontally, one set adjacent to the other, several feet high.

He hung beautiful vines around the area, creating the appearance of a tree house hung from the ceiling. With a few futon pillows and a small stereo to play soothing music, my dad originated the most comfortable study area anyone could have imagined. It was perfect for a man who preferred sitting cross-legged above eye level while spending concentrated, secluded hours buried in books. It was also a perfect place for a kid like me to, quite literally, "hang out" and play or even study on occasion.

Ultimately, my dad's persistence paid off. After many years of mental laboring, he earned his residency and later became a doctor. He has enjoyed helping people for more than twelve years now. He continues to educate himself, giving and attending medical seminars around the world.

I am so proud of my father for following his dreams. He let nothing get in his way, even though the odds were somewhat against him from the beginning. There is an old Eskimo proverb, "When you have gone so far that you can't manage one more step, then you've gone just half the distance you're capable of." My dad went the distance to create a new life for himself. Because of him, I know firsthand that it's never too late to follow a dream.

Another example is the story of my godmother, Charmaine, who found a new lease on life when she began to pursue a long-forgotten childhood dream while in her fifties. She'd always had a fascination with and love for collector's dolls as a young girl, but her large family did not have the means for such luxuries. Charmaine was one of the oldest children and spent most of her childhood caring for her younger siblings and coping with her verbally abusive mother. When she met and married Jack, the love of her life, in her late forties, he learned of her lifelong dream of having a Madame Alexander Doll collection.

Since Jack was a kind and generous man, and a strong advocate of the philosophy "it's never too late to have a happy childhood," he encouraged Charmaine to begin her collection one doll at a time. Jack even agreed to attend doll shows with her. Being an engineer, Jack's interest in the collector's dolls was motivated purely by his love for his wife and his desire to see her happy.

A number of years (and several hundred dolls) later, Charmaine has an impressive display of collector's dolls, beautifully encased in handcrafted glass and wood shelving that Jack lovingly built for her. Charmaine has named each of the dolls and takes time to "visit" each one daily. Her extensive knowledge of and experience with dolls would impress any doll collector, and she now enjoys the satisfaction of living out one of her deepest childhood desires. "Not only do I know it's never too late to have a happy childhood," Charmaine said beaming, "but it's never too late to meet the love of your life either!"

Exercises

1. Take a Class Together

Choose to learn something new together, such as a foreign language, a musical instrument, dancing, home remodeling, computer science, tennis, skiing, sculpting, golf, car mechanics, or anything that you and your child would enjoy learning together. Set aside time, and mark your calendar, to share the joys of learning while spending invaluable time together.

2. Read Together Often

Defy current statistics and make reading a family love affair. Join a book club if you are on a budget, or take out books from the library each week. Read everything from the classics, comics, humor, poetry, novels, current affairs, fantasy, history, spiritual texts to how-to books.

3. Choose an Intelligence Area to Further Develop

After going through the two self-ratings suggested, choose one intelligence area out of the seven that you would like to develop more, and have each person in your family do the same. You may want to select an intelligence area that you rated a 4 or 5 in interest level and a 1 or 2 in natural talent.

A MESSAGE FROM ALL CHILDREN ABOUT MODELING A LOVE OF LEARNING

Dear Parent or Guardian,
The ways that you approach learning
Will affect the ways that I learn.

When you avoid learning,
You teach me to be timid.
When you welcome new experiences,
You teach me to try new things.

When you give up on your dreams,
You teach me resignation.
When you set and reach your goals,
You teach me to be persistent.

So please have a love for learning
And following your dreams.
I'll have more zest for living
And a lifelong desire to learn.

CHAPTER NINE

Live Your Values

Be honest and authentic,
And live your highest values.
I'll learn from your experiences
And grow to have integrity.

A young man selling strawberries in a bushel basket knocked on the door of a neighbor's house. "Would you like to buy some ripe red strawberries just picked from my father's field?" he asked. "Yes, I would — they look delicious," said the woman at the door. "I'll take the basket inside and measure two quarts."

The boy stayed on the porch and amused himself with the woman's dog. "Wouldn't you like to come in and make sure that I'm measuring correctly?" the woman inquired. "How do you know that I won't cheat you and take more than two quarts if you aren't watching?"

The boy replied, "Ma'am, I am not worried, for you would get the worst of the deal if you did take more than two quarts."

"Get the worst of the deal?" the woman said, "How could that be?"

"Well, ma'am, if you took more than two quarts of strawberries, I would only lose the berries. You would make yourself a thief and a liar."

It All Starts with Honesty

Beauty is truth, truth beauty.

— JOHN KEATS

As the above Russian parable teaches, honesty is a priceless commodity. As much as we value sincerity and truth, few of us are as honest as we could be. We fool ourselves when we fall short of our goals, and we lie to others when we don't feel like telling the truth. We conjure up white lies to bypass confrontation, and we resist asking for feedback to avoid change.

In a long-term study conducted at Harvard University, honesty was rated as one of the top values to teach and model for our children, and one of the values most sorely lacking in our schools, along with discipline. In a survey conducted by a leading job-placement service, honesty was rated as highly as education and training among hiring companies. Applicants with strong recommendation letters and a clean record are often chosen over those with more academic training, because employers know that training is only part of the equation. Good character and trustworthiness are equally if not more valuable in the long run. An honest and forthright young person will gain the respect of her peers for her candor and the admiration of adults for her integrity.

Daryl, a twenty-eight-year-old man and family friend, recalls a high school incident that, with his father's help, taught him a memorable lesson about choosing honesty under pressure. A group of his buddies decided to go on a weekend rampage and blow up a few mailboxes in their suburban neighborhood on a Friday evening when there wasn't much else to do. Using small fireworks Daryl had in his possession, he coordinated the entire production, from the route to the getaway car. "Just a little damage done in the name of good fun," was their maxim.

Daryl didn't have any trouble enrolling three of his cronies to escort him on the late-night antic. They headed out with the intention of blowing up five mailboxes. The first was at the house of Daryl's old girlfriend — the one who dropped him like a hot potato for his better-looking friend in his sophomore year.

"Payback time, boys," he whispered as he lit the explosives and made a beeline for the car. They sped down the street and heard a loud ka-bang as they roared with laughter and turned back to see the mailbox in pieces on the road.

Next it was on to Mr. Frank's house at the edge of town. He was the stone-faced geometry teacher everybody had it in for since he showed no mercy when his flustered students flunked one of his excruciating exams. Their prank was well timed, and they shouted out victory slogans and gave each other high fives as they sped off into the night to carry out their next offense.

They drove to the home of Buzz Sanders — a twenty-one-year-old tough guy who worked nights at the local 7-Eleven. Buzz took gloating pleasure in carding the high school guys who occasionally tried to buy beer, telling them that the puppy supply store was down the street. Daryl threw in some extra fireworks and torched Buzz's mailbox.

What the boys didn't realize was that Buzz had just pulled in behind the house as they were making their getaway. Much to their surprise, a red sports car came barreling around the corner and started tailgating them. "Oh, God, it's Buzz," Daryl's pal Eddie cried out. "Lead-foot it!"

They tried to outspeed him in their old clunker, but to no avail. Buzz began to ram their back bumper with force and scream profanities out his window. "Pull over before he gets us killed," Eddie lamented. They pulled over to the side of the road with great apprehension, cringing as they waited in the car. Buzz bolted up to the driver's window demanding to know which little creep had blown up his mailbox. When nobody volunteered, he swaggered back to his hot rod and reappeared with a handgun. It was obvious he'd been drinking, and his rage was getting out of control.

"One of you slimebags better confess, or I'll blow you all away," Buzz shouted, getting unsteadier in his aim. Daryl took a deep breath and bravely jumped out of the car, putting his arms above his head. "This is all my doing. Leave the other dudes out of it. I did it. The fireworks were mine. The guys were just along for the ride."

Daryl recalls shaking so much that his teeth were chattering, and his knees almost gave out on him as he leaned up against the car. Buzz cursed him up and down and kept the gun within point-blank range. "I'm sorry, man. You have every right to be mad. I'll pay for it...I'll pay for the whole thing," Daryl pleaded.

Buzz took a few steps back and gave Daryl a blank stare. "You don't know how lucky you are that you just said that, dude," Buzz muttered, "'cause I was about to blow you away with this speedy, high-powered, whizbang squirt gun," Buzz howled as he tossed the black toy gun onto a nearby lawn.

Daryl's summer escapade cost him a lot more than the embarrassment of eating humble pie. After talking things out with his father, he realized he'd have to go to each home and apologize for his juvenile misconduct. Paying for the mailboxes, of course, would be a given. Daryl finished his humiliating rounds, with his father waiting in the car. It took all the money he'd earned from his paper route for almost a year to pay for the damage done, and not one of his buddies offered a single dime to help him out.

Now that Daryl is older and has gained some perspective, he considers the experience one of his most valuable lessons. "I learned to take responsibility and to tell the truth when I thought the stakes were really high. It made me think long and hard about the consequences of my actions after that, and I'm sure I've made better decisions because of it."

It's rare for children of any age to receive training in honesty and truth. Those who grow up to lead honest lives, like Daryl, most often learn it in their home environment. Use the list of twenty-one vital truths about honesty as a jump-start to discuss with your kids the benefits and rewards of leading an honest life:

Twenty-One Vital Truths about Honesty

1. To grow and move forward in life, being honest is a necessity.

2. Telling the truth and reaching out for help when in trouble breaks the cycle of denial.

3. Relationships that don't risk honesty cannot grow.

4. Those who fess up to their errors with humility gain the forgiveness, support, and respect of their peers, regardless of their offense.

5. People who make excuses reinforce their dishonesty and distance others.

6. Most people can sense when someone is lying.

7. Withholding the truth (lies of omission) can be an insidious form of deceit.

8. It is possible to share too much honesty, such as being too blunt or too revealing, without using good discernment.

9. Honest people have less stress because they don't have to keep track of any lies.

10. Failing to tell the truth when it will cause harm is a lethal form of deception.

11. Honesty spoken without kindness can be harsh and is often met with defense or withdrawal.

12. Kindness spoken without honesty is saccharine-sweet insincerity and is often mistrusted.

13. Honesty spoken with kindness is most effective and usually met with receptivity.

14. A dishonest person cannot be a true friend to him- or herself or to anyone else.

15. Not following through on your word with yourself or others is a form of self-deceit.

16. Withholding the truth to protect someone is usually people-pleasing in disguise.

17. You are not required to tell all just because you are asked — you have a right to use discretion and to decline when necessary.

18. The deepest deceptions of all are the ones running our lives beneath our conscious awareness.

19. People who are not open to feedback are doomed to live in self-deception.

20. Listening to the truth can be uncomfortable; not listening to the truth can be deadly.

21. Knowing the truth can set you free — even if it makes you miserable at first.

The Self-Honesty Test

The following statements represent the qualities of an honest and trustworthy person. Give yourself one point for each of the statements that are accurate reflections of you.

1. _____ I recognize when I'm in denial or fooling myself, and I tell the truth about it.

2. _____ I'm able to identify and acknowledge my weaknesses as well as my strengths.

3. _____ I have at least one peer who knows my deepest thoughts, fears, and desires.

4. _____ I have at least one mentor who knows my deepest thoughts, fears, and desires.

5. _____ I readily admit, without defense or excuses, when I make a mistake.

6. _____ If withholding the truth will cause harm, I tell the truth even when it's a risk.

7. _____ If I found something valuable that wasn't mine, I would seek the owner rather than keep it.

8. _____ I am honest about the ways I spend money, and my financial records are accurate.

9. _____ I am fair and honest in my business dealings, following the Golden Rule with all.

10. _____ I am able to tell trusted friends what's troubling me in an open way.

11. _____ I am willing to risk loss or rejection in order to be authentic.

12. _____ I've exposed anything I regret or am ashamed of to someone I trust and respect.

13. _____ I am not harboring secrets (mine or someone else's) that are holding me back.

14. _____ Honesty and telling the truth are hallmarks in my significant relationships.

15. _____ If I could get away with a crime without reproach, I'd choose to follow my conscience and be honest nonetheless.

16. _____ I am who I present myself to be. I'm not pretending to be someone I am not.

Scoring
1 to 4: Low level of honesty
5 to 8: Moderate level of honesty
9 to 12: High level of honesty
13 to 16: Superior level of honesty

Live Your Highest Values

Showing your children about God is as important as talking to them about God.

— WAYNE DOSICK

Roy, a thirty-nine-year-old African American businessman, learned that generosity was one of the greatest virtues of all when he was young. His grandparents, the most generous people he'd ever known, raised him from the time he was four. Although they didn't have much in the way of material things, they reached out to others whenever they could, generously sharing all they had.

On Sundays they'd extend invitations to community members to come for brunch after church. On holidays their home was always jam-packed with family and friends and those who had nowhere else to go. "They gave almost to a fault," said Roy. "I recall my grandmother telling a single mother to go ahead and keep the vacuum cleaner she'd borrowed from us, even though it meant we didn't have one for a while. "Dust will always be dust; but generosity will never rust," Granny would say, shrugging it off as she swept the carpet with a broom.

When one of the local neighbors, Old Man McCoy, broke his hip, the family cooked his meals and tended to his affairs for months. "He's done us a good turn on many occasions," Roy's granddad would say, "and nobody makes it in this world alone."

Roy grew to be a talented businessman, and at the age of thirty-five he succeeded beyond his wildest dreams in an Internet-related venture. His initial profit margin was well over a million dollars, with more success coming his way. Roy was torn over what to do with the profits after expenses the first year. He thought about rewarding himself with some new toys and gadgets for all his hard work, but he had all the gadgets and toys he needed. He considered making another real estate investment, but he already owned a home, and he knew in his heart that his house was enough for a single man who was rarely home.

He went on a quiet retreat at the end of the year and

examined his deepest values before making any decisions. What came to him on one of his walks through the redwoods was something he couldn't have foreseen. He found himself pondering his grandpa's unforgettable statement "Nobody makes it in this world alone." He thought about all the friends, associates, and mentors who had helped him get where he was. He realized how empty and meaningless his newfound wealth would be without the love of his supporters.

He flashed back to the generosity of his family and to the joy of those humble gatherings, and suddenly he knew what he needed to do. He began to list the people who had most contributed to his success. His diverse list included a high school English teacher, his siblings, a few grade school buddies, a number of business associates and mentors, and even an old college buddy who had lent him money to help him stay in school at a time when he couldn't make ends meet. When his list reached twenty people, he came up with a plan.

He decided to extend a cordial invitation to everyone on his list, stating that he was hosting an Acknowledgments Dinner and requesting the honor of their presence. Since a few of the people on his list were deceased, he extended the invitation to the closest remaining relative in their honor.

At the event Roy was overjoyed and told his favorite cohorts and their guests that this was the happiest day of his life. As they enjoyed their delectable meal, Roy proceeded to call each person to the front of the room one by one to acknowledge and thank them for all they had done to contribute to his success. Tears flowed, and joviality abounded as Roy's beloved family and friends learned of the special role each of them had played on his journey to success. As the final person was honored, delicious desserts were served, and each of the twenty distinguished guests received a sealed golden envelope.

Roy had the group's complete attention as he spoke: "My grandparents were the most generous people I've ever known, and they taught me well that nobody, and I mean nobody, gets there without the care and support of many people. And since nobody gets there alone, nobody should have to profit alone either. It seems only fitting for me to divide my first million-dollar profit among the most deserving — those of you who generously contributed to my life with no thought of a return."

The shocked silence was followed by merriment and cheer as twenty astonished guests opened their checks for $50,000 each. Today Roy is an up-and-coming philanthropist in charge of numerous successful ventures. Giving is a way of life for him, and for many of his associates. Those honored that evening will never forget Roy's bountiful gesture or his unrestrained happiness in sharing his good fortune with others.

Lead a Life of Integrity

This above all — to thine own self be true.

— WILLIAM SHAKESPEARE

Integrity is not a theory or philosophy. It's not an idea or concept. Integrity is the state of being complete and undivided. It is adhering to a code of values and principles. Integrity is a choice and a way of being. It can't be feigned or done halfway, any more than a skydive can be done partially. An individual who leads a life of integrity will teach much through the power of example.

Hector, a banking financer, recalls the lifelong lesson he learned about integrity when he was nine:

One of the earliest lessons I learned about integrity was from my father's shining example. My dad, Carlos, was a hardworking man supporting a family of seven on a meager income. He delivered packages and products to stores and businesses throughout Los Angeles County for over twenty years.

On days when the kids had a day off school, Dad would take a couple of us with him on his route. This gave Mom more time to get things done at home and the kids a chance to spend extra time with him. One memorable day, when Dad stopped to make a delivery at a swanky shop in Beverly Hills, my little sister, Leticia, spotted something glistening a few feet from the delivery truck. "What's that?" she squealed as we both hopped out of the truck and raced over to see what the shimmering treasure could be.

It was a bracelet with multicolored ornaments dangling from it. "Aw, it's for a girl," I said with disappointment. I was more interested in baseball cards and matchbox cars, so I gave her the treasure, even though I had gotten to it first. My sister shrieked with delight as I handed it to her.

"What did you find?" Dad asked. He examined the bracelet and muttered, "This thing is so gaudy, it must have fallen right out of Elvira's purse!" We all laughed as my sister started pretending to be Elvira, the ghoulish Halloween character.

As Leticia put the bracelet on, it slipped all the way up her arm. "That's awfully big on you," Dad said. "Let's have Cesar fit it for you in the mall." Dad's friend worked at a nearby jewelry store. When Cesar saw the bracelet, he examined it carefully with a special eyeglass. After what seemed like a long time, he let out a loud whistle and said to Dad, "Well Carlos, you might want to quit your day job now that you've acquired this little cache! This bracelet is set in platinum, and these full-scale jewels are real — emeralds, rubies, and sapphires, all laced in diamonds!"

"You're joking, right?" my dad said in disbelief. "That thing looks like it came from a toy vending machine. Are you sure it's the real thing?" Dad asked skeptically. "If this came from a vending machine, Carlos, then it must be a solid gold machine," Cesar said, amused. He wrote down what the bracelet was worth and showed it to my dad.

"Dear Lord, that's much more than I make in a whole year," Dad said, turning pale. Even though he wouldn't tell us its value, we knew it had to be a lot, because Dad started wiping his forehead, which he only did when he was nervous.

"Can I have my bracelet back now, Daddy?" Leticia whined. Dad took off his hat and scratched his head. "Please, Daddy? It was just lying on the ground all by itself." "I'm sorry, honey," Dad said. "The bangle belongs to someone who is probably missing it very much right now."

At that moment I piped in to object, "But Dad, we should sell it! We could get a pool, a house, or a new car with all that money." "Hold on, Hector. We couldn't get all of that — and even if we could, it doesn't belong to us. Someone is probably looking all over the place for this bracelet right about now."

Dad consoled Leticia by letting her pick out a special jewelry box from Cesar's store, and we headed home. The whole drive back, I was torn and questioned my father's judgment. "Dad, the person who owns this is probably really rich and can buy another one. We could use the money a whole lot more, and we're the ones who found it. What about 'finders keepers, losers weepers'?" I asked, trying to state my case convincingly.

"That's not the point, son," Dad said, shaking his head. "Finding the owner is the right thing to do, Hector, and that's what we're going to do," he said with authority in his voice. "When you take money that isn't yours, it's not a clean deal — and dirty money pollutes the soul." I could hardly argue with that; but nor could I stop thinking about all the ways that we could spend a whole year's salary!

When we got home, Mom knew the moment she laid eyes on the bracelet that it was the real thing. She insisted that we keep it out of harm's way until the owner could be found. Dad posted a couple of ads near the shop, and within twenty-four hours an elderly lady claimed it. The woman came with papers in hand to prove her rightful ownership, and trembling, she threw her arms around Dad. "I can't express my gratitude to you folks enough," she spoke through her tears. "You have returned a family heirloom I was carrying to have appraised. My hands are a bit unsteady, and my eyesight isn't so good anymore. I must have dropped it out of my purse and failed to take notice," she said sheepishly.

"My great-grandmother passed down this bracelet to me, and it's been in a bank deposit box for many years. My husband has been very ill for a while, and his insurance policy is no longer covering the expenses. This treasure may be the one thing that keeps my husband alive," she said wistfully.

My dad glanced in my direction, but I couldn't meet his eyes — I was too ashamed. As it turned out, my father's choice to be a Good Samaritan had helped an ailing man receive the medical care he direly needed. Dad's choice had a powerful impact on his family as well. When his decision was challenged, he took the road less traveled and did what he felt was right. Dad chose to live up to his values instead of being greedy. To us, he was a hero for that.

Dad's efforts didn't go without reward. Soon after the lady returned with her husband, who was receiving treatment and feeling much better. They presented my father with a check for $10,000 as a way of saying thank you. Dad refused the check a number of times, until the kind woman noticed Mom's old sewing machine in the corner. When she found out that Mom did some tailoring on the side to help pay the bills, she insisted that the money be used to buy a new sewing machine, and anything else that might be needed in the house.

My parents finally accepted the money. With it, Mom got a brand-new sewing machine, Dad bought some tools for repairing his truck, and our family went on a summer vacation for the first time! They put some of the money into an investment, and five years later, Mom and Dad had saved enough of a down payment for a modest home.

Today my Dad is not a wealthy man, but he is one of the richest men I have ever known. Every dollar he's ever spent has been clean money, and his integrity is still solid gold.

Make Regular Integrity Checks

I'm not better than one single person out there. But I know one thing for certain. I am better than I used to be.

— WAYNE DYER

We tune up our cars and change the oil at regular intervals to keep our engines clean and in excellent working condition. We clean our homes regularly to keep dust, dirt, and bacteria at a minimum. We arrange our important paperwork to keep it well organized, yet many of us are not nearly as judicious when it comes to checking up on our integrity. We may place a higher value on keeping our word than we do on changing our oil, but chances are that we do not take an integrity check at regular intervals.

There are three areas in which we exercise integrity daily: with ourselves, with others, and in relation to our values. By checking in and asking ourselves the following questions frequently, we can raise our integrity level and model excellence for our children:

1. Am I keeping my word with myself?
2. Am I keeping my agreements with others?
3. Am I being true to my highest values?

The Integrity Tune-Up

Examine the most significant areas of your life and check your integrity level. Write down any and all of the ways you may not be keeping your agreements or being true to your values in the following areas:

Self

Family

Friends

Love relationship

Community

Career

Fitness and health

Play and recreation

Spirituality

Clear up any areas in which you could use more integrity. Tell the truth, apologize, make a plan, make amends, surprise someone, give an acknowledgment, or do whatever is necessary to restore your integrity. Do an integrity tune-up every three months or so.

Share Life's Most Valuable Lessons

One of the most valuable lessons I've learned is that faith, freedom, and family are three of our greatest gifts.

— MARIE FITZPATRICK

One of the great wonders that human beings share is the capacity to self-reflect. With the gift of our immeasurable intelligence, we can reflect on our lives, on what's working and what isn't, and which values we consider the most significant. This simple knowledge, once acquired, allows us to grasp life's most valuable lessons and to pass them along to others. When we begin to understand and abide by these fundamental laws, we acquire what we need to "pass go and collect two hundred dollars" on the Monopoly board of life.

Until we reach that point, life is often a struggle, and we repeat the same old ineffectual patterns. Most of us have never taken courses in the most important subjects, such as faith, optimism, self-discipline, setting and achieving goals, ethics, stress management, persistence, integrity, people skills, and life management. Most of us randomly pick up what we know from a myriad of influences. A lucky few are mentored by those who are willing to share the most valuable lessons they have learned.

My mother has spent a lifetime studying the lessons of life and imparting them as a teacher and writer. I've attended some of her speeches over the years, and I've watched her write each of her articles and books. But what's influenced me the most have been the honest dialogues we've shared about our life lessons over the years. Diana has shared her greatest victories and most distressing mistakes, and what she has learned from them. She's been honest enough to admit her weaknesses, and bold enough to own her strengths. She invites feedback about her character from those she is close to. When we've gone through a challenge of any sort, she's usually the first to say, "What can we learn from this?" When experiencing success, she is the first one to celebrate the steps that led up to it. Her willingness to be candid and share her life lessions with me has made a real difference, and it's something that I believe children most want to learn more about from their parents.

Exercises

1. Practice Telling the Truth with Kindness

Practice telling the truth in a kind way with everyone you speak to. Take your time, watch your tone of voice, and choose your words carefully. Remember that honesty without kindness is not well received, whereas honesty with kindness invites receptivity. You'll be amazed by the improved relationships that result from this simple and honest approach.

2. Do an Integrity Tune-Up

Go through the nine items listed above in the integrity tune-up, and clear up anything that is incomplete. Tell the truth, apologize, make a plan, make amends, give an acknowledgment, or do whatever is necessary to restore your integrity.

3. Take the Self-Honesty Test

Take the time to be completely honest with yourself, and take the self-honesty test on page 139. Make it a goal to improve your level of honesty in those areas where you did not receive a point.

4. Share Your Deepest Values and Greatest Life Lessons

Set a goal to talk to your children often about the values you find most significant, and talk about why they are significant. Think about the most important life lessons you've learned thus far and share them with your children. The most significant gifts you will ever pass along to your offspring are the cherished insights and priceless lessons it has taken you a lifetime to acquire.

A MESSAGE FROM ALL CHILDREN ABOUT
VALUES AND INTEGRITY

Dear Parent or Guardian,
The principles you live by
Are the standards I will emulate.

When you act from dishonesty or greed,
You teach me to be deceitful.
When you act from fairness and truth,
You teach me to be honest.

When you fall short of your values,
You teach me weakness of character.
When you live by the values you keep,
You teach me to be consistent.

So please make responsible choices
And be accountable for your life.
I'll learn to have integrity
And build strength of character.

CHAPTER TEN

Be of Service

Teach me to be of service
And to honor the differences in others.
I'll learn generosity of spirit
And embrace all walks of life.

Generosity of spirit, when shared as a family, can lead to life-changing experiences. Children who learn to step out of their own lifestyles to serve those from a different walk of life are enriched beyond telling. Their perspective changes, and pre-conceived notions about other cultures and races are altered to include understanding and rapport. Making the time to be of service as a family generates a legacy of love that will be passed down for many generations to come.

Fifty-year-old Terri has many fond childhood memories of serving various charities with her family. Her mother was a school secretary and her father a high school teacher, and while they didn't have much money, with four children to raise, they always gave of their time and resources to better the lives of those around them. Terri's mother called their service projects "angel ventures" and blocked off one or two half days a month for these projects, which was no small task for a family of six to do. For the kids, venturing off with mom and dad was an adventure, not an activity to be dreaded. Terri's parents made it fun by playing games while in transit, and the family took photos or video footage of each experience when appropriate.

Holidays always included an element of service for Terri's family. On Thanksgiving mornings, they would take an early shift at the local soup kitchen, preparing food and helping to feed the hungry a delicious holiday meal. At Christmas, Terri and her siblings would rummage through their books, toys, trinkets, and clothing and fill several boxes with barely used nice things to bring to a nearby shelter, since there are always more women and children staying in shelters over the holidays. One of their favorite activities was singing holiday songs at the local hospitals and nursing homes, bringing along their trusty mutt, Melvin, who was always dressed up to look like a doggie-elf.

During the summer months, they would often travel for a week or two to another part of the world, such as South America, volunteering for Greenpeace, one of Terri's father's favorite causes. Her mother especially loved involving the family with the Make a Wish Foundation. They always loved seeing the sparkle in an ailing child's eyes while helping to make his or her long-awaited wish come true. The family usually helped in small but meaningful ways, such as greeting a family at the airport or pushing a child in a wheelchair at an event.

As a child, Terri assumed that all families did this sort of service work. It wasn't until she was an adult that she realized how truly blessed she was to be raised in such a socially conscious family. She learned something at a young age that many don't learn until much later in life — how fulfilling it is to give to those in need.

"It's tremendously rewarding to give charitably from the heart for no reason other than to be kind to someone in need," she stated. "It's infectious as well — to the degree that we touched another person's life, our hearts seemed to fill with an equal amount of joy. Anytime we helped others, we brought that good feeling home with us. We'd find ourselves doing nice things for each other more often, and we'd instinctively help out in the community more, such as helping an elderly person on or off a bus, picking up groceries for a neighbor, or shoveling snow for an ill neighbor."

Her family remains very close to this day and share many amazing memories. "In giving of ourselves," Terri reflects, "we shared something larger than life. It's been a real privilege to be an 'earth angel' and one of the most valuable things I've learned and passed on to others in my life."

Choose a Cause
and Take a Stand for Change

Not everything that is faced can be changed,
but nothing can be changed until it is faced.

— JAMES BALDWIN

When forty-six-year-old Leslie was going through an unwanted divorce, she receded into a deep depression, finding it difficult just to manage her everyday affairs and to attend to her teenaged son's needs. Week after week, she'd try to move through her immobilizing loss, without much success. Then she came upon a television special about Habitat for Humanity. She felt strangely ignited afterward and decided to do something for the world to lift herself out of her dark fog.

Being in the public eye in her profession, she began to enlist corporate donations toward meeting her goal: building more houses in a remote part of Brazil at one time than anyone had ever done in Habitat's history. Her natural enthusiasm for the cause brought more funding than expected, and over the following Christmas season, Leslie, her son, and a group of friends and associates built a record number of homes for a group of very grateful Brazilians. Leslie feels it was one of the most significant turnarounds in her life and attributes her self-renewal to choosing to be of service.

When twenty-two-year-old Rosita and her fourteen-year-old sister, Concepción, lost their mother to a rare form of cancer, they were devastated. Their father had passed away a few years before, and they felt very much alone in the world. They promised their dying mother, who had been passionately involved in women's causes, that they would carry the torch and not give up on life. Soon after, they became aware of a woman from Bangladesh on a powerful mission. Her name was Nasrine Hucks, and she was the leading spokeswoman in her country on behalf of "acid violence survivors" (women who have endured acid being forcefully poured on their faces by angry men — usually spurned suitors or enraged husbands who have not received their full dowry from their in-laws). Rosita confessed:

When I first became aware of the horrific repercussions of pain and permanent scarring for life that these young women faced, I felt completely overwhelmed. All I wanted to do was turn away out of denial that anything this bad could be going on in the world. But then I remembered my promise to my mother, and I began to experience a radical transformation in my outlook.

These faceless and marred young women became as angels to me, troubadours for the power of the soul to radiate through even a grossly deformed face. I began to see the act of acid violence itself as a massive crying out for love, and wondered if my mother was lending me this perspective from a higher dimension. I was no longer hopeless and helpless as before, but instead filled with a sense of true caring for all involved...both for the perpetrators, who are victims of their own violence, and for the victims themselves, who suffer unspeakable physical and emotional pain.

From this clear state, I was able to enlist the help of my younger sister and of a number of women's coalition groups, whom I am influencing to support the ending of this unconscionable act. My sister and I have plans to go to Bangladesh in the near future. Taking on this cause has been very healing for both of us, something we're sure our mother would be proud of.

There are so many ways to serve, and there's no time like the present. Below is a starter list, organized by category, to help you and your children explore the many organizations that would welcome your time, energy, and donations with open arms. Make it a weekly or monthly goal to learn more about an organization that interests you, and become aware of the many ways there are to serve:

Animals

Global Stewards — www.globalstewards.org
The Humane Society — www.hsus.org
World Animal Network Directory — www.worldanimalnet.org

Babies

Newborns in Need — www.newbornsineed.org
Faith House — www.faithvillage.org
March of Dimes — www.marchofdimes.org

Children

Advocates for Youth — www.advocatesforyouth.org
Boys and Girls Club of America — www.bgca.org
International Rescue Committee — www.theirc.org
The Make a Wish Foundation — www.makeawish.org
The Nelson Mandela Children's Fund —
      www.mandela-children.org
The Omega Boys Club — www.street-soldiers.org
UNICEF Children's Fund — www.unicef.org

Community

American Red Cross — www.redcross.org
The Hunger Project — www.thp.org
Peace Corps — www.peacecorps.gov
Salvation Army International Headquarters —
      www.salvationarmy.org
Volunteers of America — www.voa.org

Environment

Audubon Society — www.audubonsociety.org
Earth Share — www.earthshare.org
The EnviroLink Network — www.envirolink.org
Green Peace — www.greenpeace.org

The National Environmental Directory —
   www.environmentaldirectory.net
The World Environmental Organization — www.world.org
The National Resources Defense Council — www.nrdc.org

Family and Housing

Family Violence Prevention Fund — www.endabuse.org
Habitat for Humanity — www.habitat.org
National Casa Association — www.nationalcasa.org
National Coalition for the Homeless —
   www.nationalhomeless.org
National Organization of Parents of Murdered Children —
   www.pomc.com

Health

American Foundation for AIDS Research — www.amfar.org
Center for Disease Control — www.cdcfoundation.com
Hazelden Foundation — www.hazelden.org
Operation Smile — www.operationsmile.org
Walden House — www.waldenhouse.org

Women

Avon Breast Cancer Awareness Crusade —
   www.avoncrusade.com
Mom 2 Mom — www.mom2mom.org
The National Council of Women's Organizations —
   www.women'sorganizations.org
National Domestic Violence Hotline — www.ndvh.org
Women for Women Intl. — www.womenforwomen.org

Overcoming Limiting Beliefs about Service

Most of the things worth doing in the world
had been declared impossible before they were done.

— LOUIS BRANDEIS

Many of us have good intentions of serving the world but find ourselves putting it off for next month, next year, or some vague time down the road when we have "more time." The trouble with this approach is that more often than not, the time never materializes. As a result, our children grow up never having done any hands-on service work in the world, and we miss out on sharing an invaluable experience together as a family — giving back to the community and the world.

If we look a little below the surface, we may discover that our decision to shy away from service work is based on one or more unconscious beliefs, or mind-sets, that are immobilizing us without our awareness. Go through the following checklist as a family and check the faulty thoughts and beliefs that may be affecting your ability to act:

Checklist of Common Limiting Beliefs about Service

1. _____ I'm too busy to help out.

2. _____ I'm not comfortable around the sick or needy.

3. _____ I'm just one person and can't really make a difference.

4. _____ I'm not a joiner and don't trust most organizations.

5. _____ I don't have anything worthy to contribute.

6. _____ I'll help out next year when I have more time.

7._____ I have enough of my own problems.

8._____ Being around the less fortunate depresses me.

9._____ I'd rather just send a check.

10._____ I find unfamiliar people and groups intimidating.

11._____ I was once a volunteer and didn't like it.

12._____ I might be pressured into giving too much.

Take on these limiting beliefs one at a time and challenge them. Discuss the origin of each mind-set — how it was passed along and what you can do to make an attitude adjustment. This activity alone is educational to do as a family. Know that those actively lending a hand have had many of the same limiting mind-sets, but in their desire to give back to the world, they somehow overcame their resistance to reach out and help others.

For many, giving back to the community is considered a civic responsibility, a viable way to express *gratitude-in-action* for all the gifts they have received. There are few things more important to teach our children than generosity, and there is no way to be more generous than to give our time, love, and care to those in need.

Small Miracles of Service You Can Contribute to the World

The true measure of life is not its duration, but its donation.

— PETER MARSHALL

Mother Teresa said, "We may not all be able to do great things, but we can all do small things in a great way." Mini-miracles of service are small acts of love, many taking an hour or less, that make a world of difference to someone in need. Taking action in small, meaningful ways teaches kids that being of service is a vital part of life.

The following list offers some suggestions for doing a few small things in great ways:

1. Donate your airline frequent flyer miles to Miracle Flights for Kids, an organization that flies sick children to treatment centers (www.miracleflights.com), or donate unwanted foreign coins (such as pounds, yen, or euros) the next time you fly American Airlines overseas. It will be donated to Change for the Good, which supports the United Nations Children's Fund, helping children in more than one hundred and sixty countries.

2. Gather unwanted but usable items from around your home, such as clothing, videos, books, toys, old phones, computers, and sports equipment. Give the clothing, books, videos, and toys to a homeless shelter, and the phones, computers, and sports gear to a school.

3. Donate luggage, backpacks, and gym totes to a foster-family agency, since many children going to foster homes arrive with their clothing in paper bags.

4. Give hats of all sorts to the American Cancer Society ([800] ACS-2345). They will give them to children who have lost their hair because of chemotherapy.

5. Donate used musical instruments to a local school with at-risk students who would not otherwise have a chance to take a music class.

6. Give your used golf clubs to the Golf Clubs for Kids program, sponsored by the Professional Golfers Association. They will be used to introduce young people to golf who could not afford to play otherwise.

7. Donate old cellular phones to Bell Atlantic Mobile (www.bam.com). They will recycle the phones by reprogramming them to dial 911 at the touch of a button to help community safety patrols have direct access to police support.

8. Register as a family at www.igive.com, an online shopping mall that donates up to 12.5 percent of the value of the purchases you make at their website to the charity of your choice. You can make a donation in your name without making any purchases by registering to be a free member, and igive.com will make a one-time donation of $2 to your favorite charity. This is an easy and rewarding way to help nonprofit organizations as you shop for necessities and save time.

9. Beginning on November 1 of every year, you can purchase new toys online at eToys (www.etoys.com) with a Visa card and save 50 percent off retail when donating toys to Toys for Tots. More than fifteen thousand toys are donated each year by families who make it an annual tradition.

10. Donate newspapers to animal shelters. They will be shredded and used as bedding for rescued animals. Help take the animals for walks, and keep the phone number of the local Humane Society handy in your car in case you spot an injured animal.

11. Check out local groups offering certification programs that allow you to take your trained pet on

a leash to visit those who are ill in hospitals or convalescent centers.

12. Save your pennies, nickels, dimes, and quarters and locate a Coinstar change counting machine. The bright green machines automatically calculate how much change you have and convert it to paper money. Donate the money collected to a favorite charity. Call (800) 644-2646 or visit www.coinstar.com to locate the nearest machine. This is an excellent way for the very young to feel they are making a difference.

13. As a family, write an email to elected officials expressing your concerns or offering acknowledgments. For kids, this is a wonderful lesson in civic responsibility. Make sure to ask for a reply.

14. Find out what stores in your community participate in Five Percent Days — a special day each month when 5 percent of the day's total sales benefit a local charity. Grocery stores, drugstores, and household stores are often involved. By shopping on that day, you can get all your shopping done and help raise thousands of dollars for worthy causes.

15. Donate your used calendars to Friends Outside, a nonprofit organization that serves prison inmates by using old calendars to create decorative boxes. Send calendars to Box 3905, Santa Rosa, California 95402. Send your used holiday cards to St. Jude's Ranch for Children. This nonprofit residence for neglected kids gives them the opportunity to earn extra money by recycling the front sides of greeting cards. Send to 100 Jude's Street, Boulder City, Nevada 89005.

16. Give children an age-appropriate allowance each week, putting aside 5 to 10 percent of the total amount for an annual donation to a cause of your child's choice. Make sure to involve your child in writing the check and mailing or hand-delivering the gift. Let your children know what organizations you support each year and why.

Find the Good in Those Different from You

The true measure of a person can be found in the way he treats others who can do absolutely nothing for him.

— ANONYMOUS

When we encounter a disabled individual, many of us respond with a simultaneous sense of empathy and withdrawal. When we are young and have a natural instinct to stare, we are corrected and told it's rude. Often this scolding results in a sense of shame over our natural curiosity to explore that which is different from us. As we mature, we are programmed to look away rather than extending and getting to know someone who looks or acts different. This isolates us from one another, preventing the richness of getting to know someone unlike us. Ask anyone who has spent time with someone with cerebral palsy or Down syndrome what the experience has been like, and they will tell you it has opened them up to a world of humanizing experiences.

Sarah, a college senior, and her brother, Roy, a high school freshman, both started volunteering for the Special Olympics, with their father's encouragement, when they were children. One of their fondest memories that deeply touched them occurred at a summer tournament.

A few years ago, at the Seattle Special Olympics, nine contestants, all physically or mentally disabled, assembled at the starting line, preparing to run the 100-yard dash. At the gunshot, they all started out — not exactly in a dash, but with a relish to run the race to the finish line. All, that is, except for one little boy, who stumbled and fell almost as soon as he put his foot down. He tumbled over a couple of times and landed flat on his back. He lay there stunned for a few moments, and then began to cry.

The other eight runners heard the boy's faint cry in the distance. Each one of them began to slow down and look back. Then, within a matter of seconds, not one, not two, not four, but all eight of them turned around and went back — completely breaking the rules of the game to help their fellow runner. They huddled close around the sobbing boy and reached out to assure him that he was okay, patting his head, brushing him off, and helping him up.

One girl with Down syndrome kissed him on the cheek and said, "This will make it better." Then, slowly but surely, all nine of them linked arms and walked in a long horizontal line, smiling all the way to the finish line.

Everyone in the stadium stood up roaring and cheering. The applause went on for several minutes, as the nine contestants held up their arms together in victory. "People who were there are still telling the story," Sara said. "Perhaps it's because deep down, we all know that what matters in this life is something much more than winning for ourselves. What matters most is helping others win, even if it means slowing down and changing our course. The mentally and physically handicapped contestants taught everyone this on that memorable day in a way that none of us will ever forget."

Introduce a Child to Leadership through Service

I do not know what your destiny will be;
but I do know that only those who have sought
and learned how to serve will be truly happy.

— ALBERT SCHWEITZER

To involve a young person in volunteerism and being of service at an early age not only teaches generosity but also supports that young person to mature into a well-balanced, contributing member of society. Young leaders have a confidence that comes from the satisfaction of serving and the realization that their efforts really do count.

Jon Wagner-Holtz founded Kids Konnected, Inc., a cancer support group for kids, when his mother became ill with breast cancer. Jon was still in grade school, and he couldn't find a support group for kids going through the same thing, so he started a hotline in his home that kids could call and get support anytime they needed it.

Jon started out receiving a $283 grant from a cancer foundation. Now, just a few years later, Kids Konnected has an annual budget of $150,000, with chapters in twelve states. Al Gore mentioned Jon's organization at a conference for health care professionals, saying that Jon's organization was a "model of financial efficiency." As a result of this success, Jon's next aspiration is to become the youngest congressman in United States history. His more immediate goal is to train a young member to take over as CEO while he attends college so that the organization can continue to be run by kids, for kids.

When Amber Coffman founded Happy Helpers for the

Homeless, she was inspired by her many years of helping out at homeless shelters with her mother. She discovered that the kids whom she met at the shelters were just like any other kids, and she made friends with many of them. Now that she is a teenager, she and a group of volunteers, mostly teens, meet with local markets and restaurants every Friday to pick up food donations for her organization. Every Saturday morning, she and a host of teens prepare nutritious lunches and distribute them to hundreds of people who "need to be loved." She hasn't missed a weekend in over five years: "It's where my heart is." Her dedication won the attention of Mother Teresa, who invited her to come to India shortly before she passed away. Amber has learned at a young age that she has tremendous potential to serve those in need. Her next dream is to be the director of a homeless shelter.

What these young leaders have in common is the capacity to identify a need and fill it, and the enthusiasm to enroll others in their cause. While most children will not take it on themselves to initiate an organization or a movement, all children can develop many of the leadership traits that Jon and Amber have developed by doing some form of service work.

Below are some of the key qualities found in young people who have experienced the fulfillment of serving the world in meaningful ways. Most of them are exposed to service through parents, guardians, teachers, or mentors:

Key Traits of Young Leaders Making a Difference

1. They are passionate about contributing to the world in ways that matter.

2. They have real-world experiences in serving others, often through their families.

3. They exhibit minimal or no use of alcohol, cigarettes, and drugs.

4. They are less dependent on their peers for approval and a sense of belonging.

5. They are seekers of information and knowledgeable about causes they care about.

6. They are able to motivate others, including their peers, to take action.

7. They are confident in themselves with an awareness that their efforts count.

8. They are persistent in their endeavors.

9. They are hardworking with endless enthusiasm for the cause at hand.

10. They have a vision of what the future holds for them.

Focus on How Much You Can Give

We make a living by what we get.
We make a life by what we give.

— WINSTON CHURCHILL

Imagine what would occur if the majority of us were more focused on how much we can give away in a lifetime rather than on how much we can get. Actor Paul Newman understood this well when he started his food company, Newman's

Own, in the late 1970s. Initially he decided on a whim that instead of just giving away his homemade salad dressing at Christmas, he'd make it available in a few local stores. Much to his surprise, the product was enthusiastically received, with overwhelming requests for more products and wider distribution.

What started as a side business quickly escalated into a full-fledged operation. Paul and his business partner created a tagline for their company — *shameless exploitation in pursuit of the common good.* Their business quickly became a big player in the food industry. Their approach to charity was decidedly different from the onset, with 100 percent of all profits generously donated to various charities, with the goal of giving away as much as possible to better the world. To date, they have contributed more than $150 million to more than two thousand charities worldwide. This generous act of service has spurred other philanthropic endeavors to spring up, with leaders donating large portions of their profits to worthy causes.

"How much can I get in a lifetime?" is a question that many of us spend our energy relentlessly trying to answer, only to find at the end of our lives that our golden moments have always involved helping others. To step onto the playing field of "unreasonable generosity," as Paul Newman has so eloquently modeled, begin asking the question "How much can I give away in a lifetime?" The answer may surprise you.

Exercises

1. Choose a Family Cause

Find something that the whole family can support through donating time, support, or funding. Stay up on the issues at hand and share discussion and brainstorming on what is needed to reach the goals of your chosen cause.

2. Contribute a Mini-Miracle of Service Each Week

Take fifteen to thirty minutes a week to perform a small act of service. Begin with a few of the ideas provided in the mini-miracles of service list, then graduate to making your own list. Include random acts of kindness and helpful ways to reach out to others every day.

3. Ask, "How Much Can I Give Away?"

Often this includes giving to oneself, one's family and friends, the community, and the world.

A MESSAGE FROM ALL CHILDREN ABOUT
BEING OF SERVICE

Dear Parent or Guardian,
The ways that you serve and treat others
Will have a great influence on me.

When you are intolerant of others,
You teach me to be judgmental.
When you honor each culture and race,
You teach me to be accepting.

When you overlook the less fortunate,
You teach me to be apathetic.
When you reach out to those in need,
You teach me the value of giving.

So please have the heart to be helpful
And compassionate to those in need.
I'll learn to lend my heart and hand
And make the world a better place.

CHAPTER ELEVEN

Have Faith and Optimism

Focus on what's going right
And have faith during troubled times.
I'll learn the skill of optimism,
With gratitude for each new day.

Faith is a function of the heart and soul — an abiding belief in the unseen. It is a deep knowing in things the mind cannot grasp and the senses cannot touch. Faith supplies staying power, providing conviction when things appear impossible. Every noble work or deed that has ever been accomplished is rooted in the power of faith. Faith led the early pioneers to traverse the Wild West, Leonardo da Vinci to believe in a flying machine, Amelia Earhart to fly solo across the Atlantic, Columbus to discover the West Indies, Democritus to ponder the wonders of the atom, Madame Curie to discover radioactivity, and Albert Einstein to propose the unified field theory.

Although faith is invisible, its effects are radiantly apparent to all. Many of the world's greatest leaders have exerted great faith under duress, causing a ripple effect of increased faith in all the lives they touch. Maya Angelou, renowned poet, author, and spokeswoman for justice and peace, experienced the trauma of her son being in a serious car accident when he was a young adult. Maya devotedly stayed by his bedside night and day, praying for his well-being with the faith that her son would one day be restored to perfect health. His healing process was slow and painful, and at one point the doctors broke the news to Maya that her son would never walk again. Maya would have nothing of this limiting decree, responding to the doctors, "What do you know? . . . I've gone to a higher authority, and I know that my son will walk again." Over time her son's health was entirely restored, and he now leads a productive, healthy life. With tears in his eyes, he says, "My mother's faith is what made me well."

Faith Is Our Greatest Resource

A little faith brings your soul to heaven;
a lot of faith will bring heaven to your soul.

— DWIGHT MOODY

In the late 1990s Maha Ghosananda, a Cambodian Buddhist leader, was determined to bring attention to the serious problem of the land mines that are dangerously scattered throughout his country. He had witnessed firsthand hundreds of Cambodians, including children, lose limbs by unsuspectingly stepping onto one of the many thousands of land mines that remain as dark remnants of the war. He elected to walk across his country over the most dangerous land mine "red zones" in powerful protest of this intolerable condition. To the incredulity of his followers and the rest of the world, he pilgrimaged across the entire country and came out unscathed. His faith in his purpose far surpassed any fear he may have had. Maha's astonishing trust gained the notice of many global leaders, who have rallied in support of his cause ever since.

Sonia Jacobs, a woman in her late forties, was falsely accused of a crime, along with her beloved husband, more than twenty-five years ago. She witnessed her innocent husband get the death sentence and spent the next twenty-two years of her life in prison. And she was forced to let her three precious children go, to be cared for and raised by relatives.

Throughout the never-ending weeks, months, and years of gray walls and an austere life without her family, Sonia never lost faith in "finding and living her life purpose." While in prison she was convinced she had a calling and wanted to help her fellow inmates in some way. Many of them were irate and bitter over their life predicaments, unable to get past their pain. Sonia began to teach forgiveness workshops to the women there, who were immensely appreciative. Because of Sonia's powerful work, many of them experienced liberation from anger, as well as a newfound serenity and camaraderie among themselves.

When Sonia was finally released and reunited with her children, they were all grown adults. Instead of lamenting the lost years that could never be replaced, Sonia continued to practice her faith in the power of forgiveness with her beloved family. Sonia continues to teach forgiveness workshops to people of every race and creed worldwide. Her implausible faith under fire is a continual inspiration to all she meets.

Mr. Blue, a character in a novel by Myles Connolly, is a man of extraordinary faith. He is so sure of the providence and protection of a Higher Power that he is moved to give away his most treasured possessions to the less fortunate, to lie out under the evening sky each night with the inquisitiveness of a young child, and to repeatedly release gigantic bouquets of balloons with hundred dollar bills attached to them.

While it remains uncertain whether Mr. Blue is fictitious or real throughout the story, the following words written about him speak for themselves:

> It is impossible to be with him an hour without breathing a new wholesome air, charged with beauty. It is impossible to be with him and not catch the spectacular glory of the present moment. At the power of his presence, before the eloquence of his eyes, poverty, neglect, and such trifles become as nothing. One feels bathed in a brilliant and even tangible light, for it is the light he sees, and which, he would have us believe, is about us on our gallant journey toward death. All the scales of pettiness fall off the soul. The spirit stands up, clean, shining, and valiant, in an unconscious effort to match his. "Come, come," his eyes say. "Behold the perilous road! You will die, stifled with comfortability and normality, choked by small joys and small sorrows." Such is his warning as he goes. What can a man do with a fellow like that? One can catch the spirit of his life, but no writing could catch the splendor of his adventures.

Everybody Needs Someone
Who Has Faith in Them

Faith is the substance of things hoped for,
The evidence of things not seen.

— ST. PAUL OF TARSUS

Just like we need food, rest, and water, all of us need someone who can hold the faith for us, especially when we are
unable to do it for ourselves. Our friend Debra, a woman in
her mid-twenties, shares a story about the mentor who
taught her all she knows about faith:

> Growing up in Los Angeles, I inherited my parents' wor-
> ries for our safety early on. We were never allowed to walk
> home from school in case there were kidnappers on the
> loose. Our doors were always double-locked, and we sat
> down to dinner each night to hear about the violence and
> killings on the evening news. We kept up on the latest
> global calamities and sat tight in our home as though it
> were a bomb shelter.
>
> Our parents unknowingly instilled a bit of paranoia in
> my siblings and me. "Better safe than sorry!" Mom always
> said. Dad used to tell us, "Plan for the worst in advance,"
> so that we'd be prepared for anything thrown our way. I
> knew they meant well, but I sensed something was lack-
> ing in their viewpoint. It wasn't until Grandma Rose
> moved in with us that I knew what was missing — it was
> faith. Faith was Grandma's favorite word, one she used
> almost daily.
>
> Soon after she moved in, I had an upcoming soccer game
> I was very nervous about. The night before the game, I
> couldn't sleep. I went to the kitchen looking for a late-night

snack. Grandma heard me making noise and came in to join me. I told her about my anxiety and she listened, nodding sympathetically. "I have just one thing to say to you, my dear granddaughter," she said with a wink. " Have faith in yourself! You are a terrific player, and your team will gain strength from the confidence you have as you kick that ball with all your might!" The image she gave helped me to relax that night, as I fell asleep dreaming of scoring proudly for my team. Though we didn't win the game, I was honored for achieving the most points and for my team spirit.

Grandma Rose had faith in every one of us — my brother, through his college years when his grades weren't going so well, and my sister, when she needed to conquer her stage fright in order to become the leading thespian in our community. Grandma told us that every morning she prayed for us, to increase her faith in our continued health and happiness. She was a living angel in her own right. I'll never forget the way Grandma's faith came shining through when I bought my first car. My parents were worried about my driving in Los Angeles. "You shouldn't take the 405 freeway, its way too hectic," my mother would say. "Have you checked your oil and tires lately?" my father would ask with a look of apprehension on his face. I must admit that I was always a little shaky when I'd get on the road.

"Relax, dear," Grandma told me the first time she drove with me. "I know, I know — have faith, right Grandma? It's hard to have faith when they'll grant any lunatic a license to drive in the state of California," I told her. She just grinned and said, "Something much grander than a lunatic driver is keeping you safe."

The next week, Grandma Rose gave me a glittering aqua sticker that said Protected by Angels. She told me to put it on my glove box and glance at it each time I drove as a reminder that I was perfectly safe and in the hands of love. I loved the idea and made sure to call on the angels each time I started the car.

It never ceased to amaze me how impeccable Grandma Rose's timing was. Less than a week later, I was driving during rush hour when a huge refrigerator fell out of a truck and tumbled onto the road just ahead of me. When I swerved, I spun completely out of control, across four lanes, and landed squarely in the face of the busy oncoming traffic.

I was shocked and in a stupor, and didn't know what to do, until I caught a glimpse of the bright sticker. It gave me the strength to try to start my car, which, miraculously enough, worked. I knew that my only chance at survival would be to maneuver my car to the nearest shoulder of the road with lightning speed. This meant that I'd have to defy my instincts and drive straight into the oncoming traffic to pull it off. I felt a wave of fright and dread, until I heard Grandma Rose silently urging me, "Quick now, honey, you can do it!"

I scarcely missed the onslaught of approaching cars as I veered off to the shoulder of the road in record time. A car promptly pulled up behind me, and a woman got out of the car and ran to my driver's window.

"Are you all right?" the shaken woman asked. "I, I think so..." I said, still shaking as I examined myself. "I thought for sure I'd witness your death," the woman said, clutching her hand to her chest. "I watched the whole thing — the refrigerator fall out of nowhere, and the impossibly short time you had to get off the road. I don't know how you did it — I've never seen anything like it," she said wide-eyed. "You must have been protected by angels."

I was speechless and just pointed to the glittering sticker in my car. She read it aloud and said, "Where can I get a sticker like that?" I took her address and told her I knew a certain angel who could probably arrange to get one for her. As she left, we exchanged hugs and sentiments of gratitude that I had survived the incident without a scratch. Her swift arrival on the scene seemed confirmation that something out of the ordinary had occurred, and I wondered if she was acting the part of a messenger.

The highway patrol pulled up as I said my good-byes to the thoughtful woman. As I answered the questions and filled out the reports, I was filled with an uncanny sense of calm. All I could think of was my sweet Grandma Rose, whose steadfast faith undoubtedly had saved my life.

Faith Uplifts, Transforms, and Protects

Faith is an invisible and invincible magnet, and attracts to itself whatever it fervently desires and persistently expects.

— RALPH W. TRINE

Jeanette, a forty-five-year-old mother, learned much about the power of faith when her teen daughter, Amy, became involved with a wild crowd. Amy lied to her mother while seeing a boyfriend with a substance-abuse problem. Initially, Amy intended to help her boyfriend stop using heavy drugs. But instead her resistance wore down, and she began to experimentally smoke heroin, convincing herself that it was just opium and not nearly as dangerous as shooting up.

Almost overnight, Amy became addicted. Amy's boyfriend resorted to stealing money to support their growing habit, and she occasionally accompanied him. Within a short time, Amy was arrested for multiple felonies, including conspiracy to commit a crime, being an accomplice in an armed robbery, and possession of heroin. Jeanette's daughter had rapidly descended from being a lighthearted high school student with good grades to a felon who potentially faced years in prison.

Jeanette endured months of grueling court hearings, expensive attorney fees, threats from Amy's boyfriend's gang, and anguish over her daughter's predicament. She hadn't digested a meal well or slept a full night since her daughter's arrest. In some of her darkest hours, when she didn't know how to go on, Jeanette would reach out to her own mother, who would respond with, "I have absolute faith that everything is going to be okay, and that my granddaughter is not going to prison." "How do you know this, Mom?" Jeanette would plead, seeking some sort of guarantee that didn't exist. "I feel it each day as I am saying my prayers. You're both going to be okay, I just know it," her mother would say time and again, with complete conviction.

Jeanette was so close to the situation that it was difficult for her to feel anything other than numbness and shock. Nonetheless, she found her mother's solid faith comforting, and it helped her gain the strength to tell Amy she would always believe in her, even if she did have to serve time in prison. Amy cried as Jeanette went on to say that she would stand by her no matter what.

A few days before the final hearing, something came over Jeanette, and she found herself remarkably composed. "I'd done everything humanly possible, and I knew it was time to turn all of my burden and heartache over to God, once and for all." Miraculously, the scheduled judge, who was notorious for being severe with first-time offenders, was absent on the day of the hearing. Substituting for him was a judge who had a reputation for being "the most compassionate judge in the entire county," according to Amy's attorney. "I sat in the courtroom waiting for the judge to address my daughter with his verdict."

Jeanette recalls, "As he spoke, I repeated just three words like a mantra over and over — 'I trust you; I trust you; I trust you.'"

> I put my trust in God; I put my trust in the judge's decision, and I put my trust in my daughter's capacity to handle whatever was before her. It was a magnificent moment in which I placed the most precious person in my life — my only child — completely into the hands of her destiny. At that moment, I realized that my preferences had little to do with what was ultimately best for Amy, and that despite my parental concerns, all was well.
>
> The judge spoke for a full ten minutes to Amy — about the dangers of getting in with the wrong crowd, and the menace of illegal drug use to good-standing citizens. He told her openly of his uncertainty about what to do with her. On the one hand, she was a first-time offender; on the other, she had escalated into drug use and being an accomplice to a crime in a very short time.
>
> He treated Amy with dignity as he expressed his concerns. After a long pensive look, he granted her six months of drug rehabilitation and three years of probation, rather than the eleven-year pending prison sentence. "Prove to me I've made the right decision," he said looking her sternly in the eyes, "by never appearing in this courtroom again, young lady."

Jeanette reflects back on those defining moments: "My eyes welled and tears of thankfulness spilled over as I listened to the judge's favorable verdict. I stayed seated for a moment just to catch my breath. For the first time, I began to grasp the indomitable faith my mother had shown throughout this onerous time. What I could not grasp was the unbounded love of God, which shone through the courtroom in a flaming blaze as I made my exit. I made a pledge on that day to cultivate more faith and spiritual certainty in all my affairs."

Amy has been drug free since the hearing. She successfully

completed her drug rehabilitation and probation period and now, as a young adult, leads a productive and fulfilling life. Amy concedes, "The faith my family had during that dreadful time was a saving grace. Without it, I don't know where I'd be. My deepest hope is that every child in distress has someone who is holding the faith for them, especially if they are too fragile to hold it for themselves."

The Power of Holding the Field

Faith laughs at the shaking of a spear;
unbelief trembles at the shaking of a leaf.
Unbelief starves the soul, and faith finds food in famine.

— ROBERT CECIL

I was visiting with Marlo, a long-standing family friend, when the subject of her husband, Jerry, came up. "Well," she said with a sigh, "our fiftieth anniversary is coming up in just a few months. And I've realized it's been over fifty years since Jerry started drinking. I can hardly remember what he was like as the bright-eyed, sober young man I met and fell in love with over fifty years ago." She went on to say that her mentor had advised her to love him just the way he is and not to expect change at this point in his life.

"I like the first part of the equation," I told her. "But I'm wondering if you'd be willing to shift the second part and have faith in his capacity to be alcohol free and to live the life intended for him — even before he is able to do it for himself."

"Oh, I couldn't possibly do that," Marlo said incredulously. "He's been drinking for as long as I can remember. In fact, he's been drinking so long, it's just part of his identity."

"Is it really his identity," I asked, "or is it the identity that he has frozen himself in?"

Marlo fidgeted. "Well, I suppose he is very identified with the alcohol — it would be hard not to be, since he drinks every day."

"Marlo, I invite you to practice something called 'holding the field.' It is prayer in action and faith at its finest. It is the capacity *to hold someone in a field of possibilities,* where everything is possible and their highest good can take place. Do you believe you're capable of holding the field for Jerry to let go of alcohol and become all that he came here to be?" I asked.

"Not without a miracle of some sort," she said frankly.

"All right then, do you believe that I can hold the field for his complete healing and freedom from alcohol?" I asked her. Marlo said that she actually could believe in that. I invited her to think of me holding an image of Jerry's transformation whenever thoughts of his drinking came to her mind. I told her it was important to clear out any interference by switching from mental worry to "soul knowing" whenever Jerry came to mind. Even if her resistance was too great to be able to fathom the new possibility, she could imagine me doing it. "Doing this is a form of diving," I told her. "It's a tandem dive into grace." We agreed to do this for a month and to be in touch at the end of the month.

When the time came to check in with Marlo, she was overjoyed. "I don't know what to make of this," Marlo said almost breathlessly, "but Jerry hasn't had a drink in almost five days! That alone is a first! We've just returned from an event, and he didn't drink at all. Do you think this holding-the-field exercise had anything to do with it?"

"What do you think?" I asked her.

"I think this practice is a breeding ground for miracles. In the first three weeks, there wasn't much change, except within me. Every time Jerry had a drink in his hand, I'd imagine you, Diana, holding the field for him. Instead of judging him or distancing myself from him, I began to feel hopeful for no particular reason. I was even more accepting of and affectionate toward him.

"Last week, we were talking late into the night, something we haven't done in a long time, and we talked about his drinking. I told him how much I missed our early days before his chronic use of alcohol had created a gap between us. Not much was said, but Jerry hasn't had a drink in over five days now."

This was just the beginning for Marlo and Jerry. We continued for another thirty days, followed by a third round. During that time, Jerry had a few starts and stops. Almost one year later, Jerry has not had a single drink in months, and their relationship has never been better. Marlo considers it a miracle, saying, "It's almost too good to be true." I suggested that she consider it "completely good and perfectly true" instead. Marlo's willingness to change her thoughts about her husband may be the biggest miracle of all, acting as a domino effect as she supported him to leave alcohol behind and step into a whole new world.

Practice Healthy Optimism

You can't raise positive people on negative feedback.

— GERALD JAMPOLSKY

The most common view of optimism is that it's a pie-in-the-sky perspective on life. The ultrapositive optimist is pegged with phrases such as "Every day in every way, I am getting better and better." While this may pass as optimism, in some cases, it may have more to do with denial than optimism. Denial is a refusal to face reality as it is and a capacity to create a grandiose interpretation of any bleak situation.

Healthy optimism is not the absence of seeing things as they are; rather, it is the capacity to see things as they are and to identify what's working as well as what's needed. The basis of optimism does not lie in motivational phrases, but in a way of thinking and being in the world. Healthy optimism is the unrelenting pursuit of what is possible despite limitations or obstacles. Two prime qualities of healthy optimism include a focus on:

1. *What's working.* With healthy optimism we find and acknowledge the good in ourselves, others, and the world.
2. *What's needed.* With healthy optimism we seek to gain understanding and find solutions.

Parents and guardians have a tremendous mental and emotional impact on their children based on attitude alone. When we choose healthy optimism as a way of life, our children are encouraged and supported, even when making mistakes and needing correction. Kids who live with healthy optimists develop positive traits that will benefit them throughout their lives. The following examples are just a few of the interactions that a parent might have with a child in the course of a day. Note the dramatic difference in the messages conveyed to a child based on an optimistic or pessimistic approach:

PESSIMISTIC PARENTING (focuses on the negative)	OPTIMISTIC PARENTING (focuses on what's possible)
• You never listen to a word I say!	• I'd appreciate it if you'd listen to me.
• You don't have any talent in art at all.	• Maybe art isn't your thing right now.
• Your room is such a pigsty all the time!	• Your room needs your attention.
• You are such a klutz!	• Keep practicing, and you'll improve.
• Can't you ever get anything right?	• If you pay attention and stay with it, you'll get it right.
• You are just as ditzy as your sister when it comes to directions.	• You'll have to concentrate to get the directions right. You can do it.
• He is such a spoiled rotten brat.	• He could really benefit from better manners.
• You are always complaining!	• What do you suggest?
• I can't stand it when you whine!	• Please use words and talk calmly.
• That's it. I've had it with you!	• I need a break. Let's talk later.
• You were horrible in the store today!	• I want your cooperation when we're in the store.
• If you forget to do this, you'll be sorry!	• Please make sure to do it — it's important, and I'm counting on you.

Since parents have such a huge influence on their child's life, it comes as no surprise that in a long-term study conducted at Loyola University, it was found that pessimistic children almost always came from pessimistic homes. Likewise, children who were optimistic often had adults in their environment who were focused on the positive. As a child repeatedly hears what's going right or what's going wrong from a significant adult, a myriad of thought patterns gets firmly established. Pessimistic or optimistic perspectives become internalized, and a child begins to view many of life's everyday circumstances through these thought-filters. Here are a few examples:

THE PESSIMISTIC CHILD (finds what's wrong and what's missing)	THE OPTIMISTIC CHILD (finds what's working; seeks solutions)
• I'll never make friends at the new school.	• Making friends will take time and friendly effort on my part.
• My dad is the meanest dad in the world!	• My dad is in a bad mood right now.
• John probably hates me and won't want to hang out with me anymore.	• John is mad at me right now. What is my part? What can I do differently?
• I flunked the test because I'm stupid.	• I need to study a lot harder to get a better grade.
• My friends tease me to hurt me.	• My friends tease me just because they think it's cool to do.
• I'm not good at math, and I never will be!	• I'll have to work a lot harder if I want to get good scores in math.
• Everyone thinks I'm really fat!	• I'm ready to lose weight and get fit.

Since optimism is a learned skill, having an upbeat attitude will bring a positive perspective to many of life's everyday moments. Here are a few ways to do just that:

Five Ways to Develop Healthy Optimism

1. Each day, share with someone you love at least one thing that's *going right* in the world.

2. Compliment or acknowledge *three people a day.* For extra optimism bonus points, give a sincere compliment to every person you encounter!

3. Each evening, before going to sleep, ask yourself the *three optimist's questions:* What's wonderful? What's working? and What's needed in my life?

4. Pick one challenge each day and look at it from a *higher perspective.* Find the gift or lesson in it so that you can recognize it as a contribution.

5. Create a *gratitude book* for the whole family to spontaneously write in. Read it aloud together at least one day a week.

The Perils of Pessimism

No pessimist ever discovered the secrets of the stars,
or sailed to an uncharted land,
or opened a new heaven to the human spirit.

— HELEN KELLER

Sadly, America's children are in the midst of a pessimism epidemic, with frequent reinforcement coming from critical adults, bitter music lyrics, angry clichés printed on T-shirts, and movies and television shows filled with violence, murder, and deception. A fundamental task for adults is to prevent children from internalizing this insidious way of life. Pessimism is much more than a bad mood or a difficult phase. It is an entrenched way of thinking with far-reaching consequences. Pessimistic children experience resignation, poor physical health, underachievement, social conflicts, loneliness, anger, addictions, self-loathing, and diminished self-esteem.

Pessimism does not diminish with the typical ups and downs that are part of normal life. Instead, it hardens with each impediment, creating a self-fulfilling prophecy. It erodes our children's innate sense of curiosity and joy, leaving them hesitant, mistrusting, and skeptical. It is catastrophic in nature, averting new relationships, ideas, and opportunities. A pessimistic child ends up burrowing into a distant place of isolation and aloofness. We cannot protect our children from every negative influence that crosses their path, but we can examine our attitudes and choose to eradicate our own habitual negative habits in the following ways:

Five Ways to Stamp Out Pessimism

1. Play the "Go Higher" game by changing your tune each time you say something negative. For example, instead of saying, "What an awful gloomy day it is today," *go higher:* "What a great opportunity it is to stay indoors and get some things done!"

2. *Monitor your thoughts* when you are alone, and be aware when you are on a pessimistic roll. Say silently

to yourself, *switch,* and turn your thoughts from doom and gloom toward what's working or what's needed.

3. *Edit out* name-calling, swearing, and negative phrases by saying the word *cancel* aloud and allowing those around you to cancel your words aloud. Do this in fun, with the serious intention of stamping out negativity.

4. Take a *thirty-day mental diet* in thought, word, and deed by using the three techniques above. Do it with the intent to shed tons of mental weight!

5. Take a *ten-minute time-out* if you are obsessing on the negative, yelling, criticizing, or complaining. Give your loved ones permission to request a ten-minute time-out if you are unaware that you're stuck. Use the ten minutes to ask yourself, What do I need to turn this state around?

Take the Pessimist-Optimist Test

*An optimist may be wrong as often as a pessimist;
but they have a lot more fun finding out they are wrong.*

— ANONYMOUS

Are you more of an optimist or pessimist? How about your child? Many of us are a combination, while some of us lean predominantly to one side. Read through each column, and check all the qualities that you demonstrate. If both apply on a given number, check off the quality that is predominant. After you've finished, see the scoring below.

What All Children Want Their Parents to Know

A PESSIMIST	AN OPTIMIST
1. ___ Is missing healthy role models	___ Has one or more healthy role model
2. ___ Focuses on faults and weaknesses	___ Self-corrects and develops strengths
3. ___ Has poor self-regard	___ Has strong self-respect
4. ___ Assumes the worst	___ Looks for the best
5. ___ Avoids unpleasant issues	___ Gets to the issue seeking resolution
6. ___ Complains often	___ Cooperates often
7. ___ Criticizes and puts down	___ Acknowledges and builds others up
8. ___ Is curt or rude to authorities	___ Is respectful or polite to authorities
9. ___ Is closed with a guarded heart	___ Is open with a warm heart
10. ___ Is sarcastic, bitter, or cynical	___ Is humorous, upbeat, and fun
11. ___ Shuns being of service	___ Contributes to the lives of others
12. ___ Gives up easily when it gets rough	___ Keeps going with persistence
13. ___ Isolates out of pain or protection	___ Stays connected to others
14. ___ Withholds feelings; is shut down	___ Expresses feelings; is vulnerable
15. ___ Is bluntly honest without kindness	___ Is considerately honest with kindness
16. ___ Mistrusts people and their motives	___ Is open to learn of others' motives

A PESSIMIST	AN OPTIMIST
17. ___ Competes and wants to be the best	___ Competes with her personal best
18. ___ Focuses on what's missing	___ Focuses on what's working
19. ___ Fears and avoids the unknown	___ Explores and seeks the unknown
20. ___ Is prone to depression	___ Has good mental health
21. ___ Harbors anger and resentment	___ Moves through anger and progresses
22. ___ Practices little or no moral reflection	___ Aspires to strong and clear values
23. ___ Exhibits poor daily self-care	___ Exhibits good daily self-care
24. ___ Is prone to addictions	___ Avoids substance abuse
25. ___ Is lethargic and lackluster	___ Is ambitious and motivated
26. ___ Is difficult and draining	___ Is energizing and interesting
27. ___ Is careless or reckless	___ Is strong in character and likable
28. ___ Gets poor grades; lower achievement	___ Gets high grades; more achievements
29. ___ Shows poor self-discipline	___ Shows good self-discipline
30. ___ Has a negative attitude about the future	___ Has a positive attitude about the future
___ TOTAL	___ TOTAL

Tally your scores from each column, and give yourself a pat on the back for taking the time to evaluate and improve yourself.

Scoring
5 or less: Low
6–12: Moderate
13–20: High
21 and up: Very high

If you scored high in the pessimism column, consider it an open invitation to learn to find the silver lining in all your affairs. Now is the time to become a member of the "4-Ws Club," focusing on "what's wonderful and what's working" each day rather than pointing out what's awful and what's not working. If you scored high in the optimist column, your efforts are commendable! Continue to cultivate a positive perspective, and keep on soaring to new heights. You are an inspiration to many, and you bring a fresh, upbeat outlook everywhere you go.

Exercises

1. Practice Having Great Faith

Take the high road and choose to have faith in the circumstances of your life that most concern you. Activate your capacity to trust and let go. Choose to let go of the ineffectual habit of worrying, which is a futile exercise in negative meditation. Hold the field for those you love, and encourage others to have faith in troubled times.

2. Develop Healthy Optimism

Choose to develop more optimism. Pick one of the five suggestions on page 189, and stay with it until it becomes an established habit. After you've mastered one, take on another.

3. Eradicate Negativity

Choose one of the five ways to stamp out pessimism, and take it seriously enough to stay with it until there is a notable change in behavior. Enlist the support of a buddy if needed, since altering an old habit can be more challenging than establishing a new one.

4. Take the Pessimist-Optimist Test

Make it a goal to lower your pessimist score and raise your optimist score. For the brave-hearted: ask a few trusted people in your life to score you in both, and see how your scores compare.

A MESSAGE FROM ALL CHILDREN ABOUT
FAITH AND OPTIMISM

Dear Parent or Guardian,
The attitudes and beliefs that you express
Will greatly affect my perspective.

When you act out of doubt or fear,
You teach me to be mistrusting.
When you live from your convictions,
You teach me to have faith.

When you focus on finding fault,
You teach me to be pessimistic.
When you find what's going right,
You teach me to be optimistic.

So please have faith and optimism
And view me with positive regard.
I'll find the good in myself
And see the goodness in others.

CHAPTER TWELVE

Give Unconditional Love

Love me without condition,
Throughout my ups and downs.
I'll know that I am cherished
And bring more love to the world.

Loving one another is simple and gratifying when things are going well, but few things are more challenging than choosing to love in the difficult moments, when it would be so much easier to respond otherwise. We teach our children much by loving them consistently and unconditionally, and we teach them even more when we choose love over fear in the midst of challenge.

Two of my clients, Ralph and Carolyn, often bickered over money at the dinner table in the presence of their three children. One day Ralph blurted out, "Can you explain where in the world all the money has gone again this month?" "Not any more than I can explain why I love you more and more, despite the way you're acting," Carolyn answered with a smile.

The children looked up in complete surprise as Ralph and his wife found themselves chuckling, followed by an embrace. They agreed right then and there, in the presence of their greatly relieved children, to stop haggling over money, to create a monthly spending plan, and to stick to it, as their financial adviser had so adamantly recommended. With a simple act of responding to fear with a small act of love, Carolyn was able to break this unconscious pattern of fighting and reawaken her husband to their enduring love.

Elizabeth, a wonderful grade school teacher in our neighborhood, was going through a rough phase with her hyperactive class, and the situation was getting worse. One day, at a point when she normally would have started correcting students with an impatient edge in her voice or randomly given out detentions, instead she took a deep breath and reminded herself that the real reason she was a teacher was because she loved each child in her classroom. As she looked around, she saw a room full of restless, fidgety kids and said to herself, "So, this is what needs love right now."

Trivial as that moment seemed, what followed surprised her almost as much as it surprised her class. She turned to the kids and came out with, "Okay, everyone, because I love all of you this much [she spread her arms as wide apart as she could], we are going to take a much-needed love break. For the next few minutes, everyone stand up, stretch, walk around, and tell a few of your fellow students something you love about them."

Elizabeth was taken aback by her own unanticipated action — it definitely hadn't been part of her teaching plan. She was even more surprised by the results. Kids gave one another high fives and shared genuine sentiments amid the laughter. A few came up to her and gave her hugs or acknowledgments that really touched her. One of the boys who had been acting out approached her and said, "Thanks, Teach, for giving us love even when it's hard to find!"

Elizabeth realized she had received an invaluable gift and decided she would approach her students with love regardless of the upset, and she kept her word on this. As a result, she became one of the most popular and requested teachers in her district and was eventually honored as Teacher of the Year.

Sixteen-year-old Randy and his mother, Bev, were having a bitter battle over his intermittent drug use. His mom had discovered powdered speed in his pocket for the third time and was beside herself with fear for his safety and frustration over his failure to tell her the truth. After threatening to kick him out of the house and take his car away, Bev felt a wave of compassion come over her as she observed him stooped in his chair with his head buried in his hands.

"The truth is, I don't have any idea what to do about this right now," she told Randy. "But I do know that I'm going to love you very much no matter what you ever do," she said with tears streaming down her face. She said this so sincerely that Randy opened up and told his mom that he felt lost and didn't have any idea how to get through his life and his problems. She didn't say a word. She simply reached out and held her six-foot-two son in her arms as he talked of his adolescent agonies, included pain over his absent father, frustration that he didn't fit in at school, and sadness that he couldn't get the attention of the girl he'd been interested in for more than two years.

The vulnerability and love that Randy's mother expressed

to him broke the shame-blame cycle they had been in, making it safe enough for him to talk to her from his heart — a significant first step in supporting a teen caught up in drug use. Over time, they worked with a therapist and shared more heart-to-heart talks at home. Randy gathered the courage to talk more honestly with both his parents, and they learned to speak to him in supportive ways without the shame or blame. Eventually, Randy was able to kick his drug habit. Bev realizes that things took a turn for the better from the moment she spoke from her heart to her son.

My colleagues, Patricia and Vern share an act of love that has kept their relationship intact and moving forward throughout their twenty-five-year marriage. Whenever they begin to argue, they play a game called "How High-How Fast." It stands for "how high can we rise above this; how fast can we get off of it." They describe it as a way to challenge one another to step out of their own point of view and return to love.

The first one to get off of it or rise above the problem wins the game. "We adapted this idea from Albert Einstein, who knew that problems can't be solved from the same level they were created — a higher perspective is needed. This idea may seem simple, but it's far from easy, especially when resistance is high and we're both sure we're right. When the heat is on, it takes a lot to let go of the need to be right, which is always the first step needed to gain new awareness."

Patricia feels there's nothing quite as vitalizing as saying, "Let's go higher than this" or, "I know we both have something to learn from this" or to reverse roles and take the other person's point of view as a fun way to get off it. Both Patricia and Vern consider this small but significant game of theirs one of the greatest acts of love they've shared over the years, one they have passed along to their families as well.

Live at the Pace of Love

There is no remedy for love but to love more.

— HENRY DAVID THOREAU

A few years ago, I learned a profound lesson in love while attending a meeting with friends and mentors Scott and Shannon Peck, founders of the Love Center in San Diego, California. An important event was coming up, and the group was wondering if the Pecks would be able to finish their upcoming book. "You'll miss a big opportunity if you aren't done," one person offered. Another asked, "Can you commit to completing your book in time for the event?"

Scott took a deep breath, looked her straight in the eye, and without skipping a beat, he said, "What I'll commit to is this — to moving at the pace of love." There was a hushed silence, and we all looked at one another speechless. The pace of love? How simple yet profound, like love itself. Scott was committing to doing what must be done, with love not just as the final outcome but as the *only* outcome.

Imagine if parents, kids, teachers, government officials, or leaders at a United Nations meeting for that matter, did everything at the pace of love. Imagine how many more people would stop to notice the beauty in their environments, how many parents and kids might play together in the park, and how much more often we'd remember how few things really matter.

It seems a good practice to live each day at the pace of love. When losing sight of love as our one true purpose, we can remind ourselves to move to the tempo of love. It never fails to shift the day into one of much more relaxation and wonderment. It allows us to become more attentive to the things that most need love and attention that might otherwise go unattended. Of all the valuable life lessons we can impart, living at the pace of love has to be one of the most far-reaching.

The Miracle of a Love Letter

Love comforteth like sunshine after rain.

— WILLIAM SHAKESPEARE

Human beings often hold back from extolling the things they most appreciate about another until it's too late. Rather than delivering a eulogy after a loved one is gone, why not offer the praise while they are alive? The simple act of writing a love letter can be a small but life-changing event for the giver and receiver.

Jill, a forty-seven-year-old mother of two, decided to write her father a love letter for his birthday:

> I decided to write my father a letter to tell him how much I appreciated him. I told him he had always been one of the brightest lights in my life, and I included a special thanks for giving me two invaluable gifts that have stayed with me for a lifetime — unconditional love and a great sense of humor. I had some trepidation about giving my dad the letter since he tended to shy away from too much emotion. Still, I felt compelled to tell him what he meant to me here and now, rather than waiting for some future time that may never arrive. I decided to risk pride and embarrassment to tell him how I really felt.
>
> To give him some private time to read the letter, I placed it on a table in his home on the day of his birthday, and returned a few hours later. When I came back, I overheard him raving on the phone about the amazing letter

he'd received from his daughter and how much it had brightened his day. I was elated that I'd followed my intuition — especially since it was the last thing I'd ever give to my father. He died just two months after I wrote him the letter. It has brought me so much peace to know that I told my dad these things in his final months on earth. It has even made the grieving process a little bit easier.

I was so inspired by Jill's story that I decided to include a special poem in a Father's Day card to my father entitled "What I Love about My Dad." It took me all of five minutes to jot down twelve things that I loved about him. It surprised me how quickly the pen moved when I thought of some of the things I most loved about my father. After sending it, I had a deep sense of peace and satisfaction and wondered what had taken me so long to do such a simple act.

A few days later, I called my dad for Father's Day, and he practically gushed over the phone. He told me that the card was "precious" (a word I'd rarely heard him use) and that he'd already read it several times. Here is what I wrote:

WHAT I LOVE ABOUT MY DAD

He has a kind heart and a good spirit.

He prays for his children every day.

He loves my precious mother, and she knows it!

He is a wonderful, funny, lively grandfather.

He cares about everything, even if he doesn't say it.

He allows room for his children to be who they are.

He's gifted us with his great love of music, nature, gardening, birds, travel, humor, and so much more.

He loves current affairs and stimulating his mind.

He is there for others in their time of need.

He has compassion for the less fortunate in this world.

He is my God-given, wild, and wonderful Dad for all eternity!

Aviva, an innovative junior high teacher, began to add a love letter exercise to her teaching curriculum, encouraging students to write a one-page love letter to a family member, friend, or someone in the community each month. She even provided the stationery and the stamps to make it as easy as possible for her students to do. The purpose of the letter was to express love, appreciation, or gratitude to someone making a difference in their lives. At the end of the school year, each of her students had written up to nine love letters to significant people — more than most people will write in a lifetime! Many of her students continue to write love letters after leaving her class. This exercise has garnered much praise and appreciation from the community. On a number of occasions, Aviva has received heartfelt thank-yous from grateful people in letters that she will cherish for a lifetime.

Mara, a seven-year-old girl, wrote a short and sweet love letter to her mother in large purple letters and tucked it under her mother's pillow at a time when her mom was going through an illness. Her mother treasures it so much that she framed it:

Dear Mommy,

I love you deeper than the deepest ocean,
higher than the big blue sky,
and wider than the whole wide world!

I'm glad God made you to be my Mommy,
And me to be your girl.
I love you with all my heart,

Mara

The following is a letter that Marty, a forty-nine-year-old father, wrote to his fifteen-year-old son, Shane, shortly after his own father passed away without warning. In Marty's grief, he realized that he'd never had a heart-to-heart talk with his father, and that he never really knew him. He could see that he was repeating the same pattern with his own son and realized that he'd never told his son what he most loved about him. Below are the words that changed the course of his son's life:

Dear Son,

As I sit in the quiet of this late hour missing my dad and thinking about all of the things never spoken between us, I realize how much I've never told you. Old habits die hard, and I have been negligent in telling you how much you've meant to me over the past fifteen years. God only knows there's no time like the present, so here goes:

Because of you, I am more easygoing and laugh more often. Because of you, I've learned to love animals more — including rats and snakes! Because of you, I've had the fun of volunteering for your baseball team. Because of you, I have finally learned more about computers. Because of you, I get a lot more basketball practice in the driveway.

Because of you, I've had the good fortune to call myself a father, even if I've not always been such a great one. Because of you, I want to get up each day and go to work and raise you as best I can. Because of you, I thank God on my knees every day.

Please know that despite how busy I am or how tough I may seem, that I'm still learning about how to be a good father, and that I'm very proud of you, and of the man you are becoming. Most important, please know that you mean the world to me, and that I will always, always love you, even if I don't say it often enough.

With Love,
Your Dad

At first, Shane didn't say anything about the letter. But a few nights later, Marty had a knock on his door before bed. Shane just wanted to "hang out and talk a few minutes," and they ended up talking for over an hour about his grand-father's death, and some of his fears about death. In the weeks following, Marty and Shane both opened up more. One morning, more than a week later, Shane gave his dad a hug as he was rushing off to school and said, "Hey Dad, I forgot to thank you for the letter — it was cool."

Amazingly, Marty had no idea that his son had been in a depression for some time, compounded by his grandfather's death, when he received the letter from his father. And Marty had no idea that his son was considering ending his life the very day he received the letter from his dad — the letter that convinced him that maybe it made sense to hang around for a while, the letter that reminded him of something he had long since forgotten — that his dad really did love and value him. Marty's letter had more impact on his son than he ever could have imagined. Our words of love to one another are no small miracle.

Ponder What You Love Often

Love stretches your heart and makes you big inside.

— MARGARET WALKER

The many things we love and hold dear are one of the most enduring miracles gracing our lives. Though we often lose sight of these daily wonders, the things we most love are truly some of the great elixirs of life. Eight-year-old Eric and his mother, Beth, enjoy naming what they love on their morning walks with their three dogs — sometimes silently, and sometimes aloud. They call it the "What I Love" exercise. Here are a few of their small but great loves:

I love the smell of the morning air on a summer's day.

I love the sound of my dad's hearty, loud laugh.

I love getting into my bed at night when the sheets are crisp and clean.

I love the taste of a ripe avocado I've just picked off the tree.

I love the feeling of playing a new song on my violin just right.

I love the fragrant scent of tiger lilies.

I love to watch our three dogs wrestle and play together.

I love the feeling of having plenty of time in the morning.

I love putting the first colors on an empty canvas.

I love the feeling of accomplishment I have after going to the gym.

I love to ride my bike along the beach and feel the breeze on my skin.

I love curling up to hot chai tea and a good novel.

I love taking a long hike in the forest.

I love to give a random act of kindness to someone I don't know.

I love to hold a sleeping baby in my arms.

I love getting an extra-long hug from someone I care about.

I love to putter around in the garden.

I love the feeling of checking everything off my list at the end of the day.

I love receiving an unexpected card or present.

I love to watch the snow falling from my spot by the fire in my warm home.

I love having a great meal with my whole family gathered around the table.

I love the feel of the wet clay in my hands as I'm spinning the potter's wheel.

I love the peace I feel in my heart after saying my evening prayers.

I love having my hair washed.

I love to think about all that I'm grateful for when I first wake up.

There are countless things worthy of love in these short lives of ours. The more you ponder them with those you love, the more you will fill your life with what you love, and the more you'll encourage your children to do the same.

Loving a Child: One of Life's Ultimate Gifts

*We find delight in the beauty and happiness of children
that makes the heart too big for the body.*

— RALPH WALDO EMERSON

In working with adults of all ages and backgrounds, I often ask them to list what they consider to be the five greatest accomplishments of their life. Never once has the acquirement of real estate or a great investment deal hit the top-five list. Never has getting away to a great place in Bora Bora made the list. Never has a career bonus or award made the list. Without fail, loving family and others well is what makes it onto the list — and loving a child is always at the very top.

What a great accomplishment it is to truly love a child. Whether you do it as a parent, aunt, uncle, grandparent, foster parent, mentor, teacher, or beloved family friend, few things will ever reap such bounty as influencing a child's life for the better. A well-loved child will spread love into the world to the power of ten. A well-loved child will contribute talent, time, and service to the world, aspiring to make it a better place.

The twelve qualities of a well-loved child and the poem that follow serve as reminders of what we have a hand in spiritually molding as we give to the children we love so dearly day in and day out:

Twelve Qualities of a Well-Loved Child

A well-loved child is:

1. *Secure:* safe, protected, nurtured, and cared for
2. *Curious:* fascinated by new experiences, learning, and the unknown

3. *Joyful:* takes joy in life's many small and great blessings

4. *Playful:* interactive, fun-loving, and capable of playing well alone and with others

5. *Confident:* has a healthy esteem and belief in her talents and abilities

6. *Risk-taking:* overcomes fear and tries new things; takes calculated risks

7. *Resilient:* bounces back from mistakes, setbacks, and corrections

8. *Authentic:* sincere, unpretentious, and natural

9. *Trustworthy:* honest, credible, and reliable in word and deed

10. *Congenial:* good-natured, friendly, and capable of relating well with others

11. *Conscientious:* mature, aware, thorough, and diligent

12. *Loving:* caring, extending, forgiving, and loving of himself and others

Love Transforms Tragedy into More Love

Every moment is made glorious by the light of love.

— JELALUDDIN RUMI

Michael, a forty-five-year-old avid pilot and father of four, shared a unique perspective with me on the power of love to transform tragedy into greater love. Some years ago, one of his closest friends, Jack, was heading for Alaska with a few others in a private plane. He brought his teenaged son, Robbie, in the hopes of giving him the adventure of a lifetime.

After flying for a number of hours, the fatigued pilot forgot to refuel the plane at the last landing they'd make before reaching their destination. As they flew over the majestic ocean just hours away from Alaska, they ran out of gas and plummeted into the sea. The passengers were able to maneuver their way out of the sinking plane, but they were unable to rescue the pilot from the wreckage.

The traumatized survivors began to swim toward the distant shoreline amid tumultuous waves. At some desperate point in that surreal time, Jack glanced back to see that Robbie was faltering, unable to keep the pace. Without hesitation, he turned and began to rapidly swim back toward Robbie, with every intention of saving his son's life. But the forceful waves and the strain of the crash overtook them both, and in a short time, they both went under. The only survivor watched despairingly from the shoreline, losing all his cotravelers in the untimely crash of their Alaska-bound flight.

"How sad" was all that came to me as Michael finished the story with an uncanny sense of calm. "How did you ever get over this?" I asked, getting a little teary. "He was one of your best friends, and you're a pilot with three sons yourself. Can you even imagine going through this?"

"Well," he responded, "at first it was really devastating, but over time something came to me in a dream, and now I am at peace with it." He continued:

Imagine the shock of knowing that you are about to go under — to just be wiped out by these huge, fierce waves that are engulfing you. You know you are about to drown. You're just a kid, and you thought your whole life was ahead of you. You feel a wave of panic unlike anything you've ever experienced as you sense the end of your life fast approaching.

You feel alone and terrified…and then your dad appears in the distance, frantically swimming toward you — back into the raging waves with every intention of saving you. In that single moment, you have a transcendent moment with your father unlike any other — one that no one will ever know of. You catch each other's glance for a split second as you see your father frantically swimming toward you. And in that one moment, your spirits seem to speak to one another: "Dad, do you really love me so much that you'll risk your life to come back for me?"

And the answer that reverberates back is, "Yes, son, I love you so very much that I will gladly give my life if that's what it takes."

"And that is what it took," Michael said with a quiet reverence. "I have no doubt that Jack is safe and sound with his son now. Sometimes I try to imagine what that moment of absolute and total love was like for them in their last moments. Perhaps only they and the angels know. I do know one thing for sure — this is the kind of love that people live and die for. And I, for one, would surrender it all for just one moment of that kind of unspeakably selfless love. If we're lucky, we'll have a few moments like this in an entire lifetime."

Michael was able to find the love in a situation where it was most difficult to see at first. We all are called to find and celebrate love, not just in the good times, but also in the worst of times, because in the end, love is all that really matters.

Exercises

1. Choose Love in the Difficult Moments

Practice choosing to love when in fear or undergoing a challenge, and witness the transforming power of love to shed new light on situations that may seem impossible. Remind yourself "this is what most needs love right now."

2. Practice Living at the Pace of Love

Make living at the pace of love the focus of each day and each hour, and experience a whole new way of relating to life, with love as the central theme and abiding purpose of each day.

3. Write a Love Letter to Someone a Few Times a Year

Write a letter or card of love, appreciation, and gratitude to someone every few months, and have your children do the same. Include family and friends, the less fortunate, the forgotten, those in pain, community leaders, guides, mentors and teachers, and those who selflessly give with no thought of return. In time, you may find it one of the most wonderful ways to express more love.

4. Play the "How High-How Fast" Game

Practice the game of "how high can we rise above this; how fast can we get off of it" when you get caught in thinking you are right and the other person is wrong. In the spirit of love rather than competition, see who can be the first to come into a higher perspective and get out of the shame-blame cycle, returning to love, respect, and positive regard for one another.

A MESSAGE FROM ALL CHILDREN ABOUT
THE POWER OF LOVE

Dear Parent or Guardian,
What you teach me about love
Will be etched in my heart forever.

When your love is conditional,
You teach me to feel unlovable.
When your love is enduring,
You teach me that I am lovable.

When you are distant or cold,
You teach me to close my heart.
When you are caring and warm,
You teach me to be openhearted.

So please tell me you love me
In all that you say and do.
I'll know the meaning of love
And be devoted to you in return.

ACKNOWLEDGMENTS

A heartfelt thanks to H J Kramer and to New World Library for their ongoing support and commitment to publishing books that make a difference. Special thanks to Kristen Cashman and Mimi Kusch for their outstanding editing and willingness to go the extra mile. Diana thanks Julia for being a brilliant coauthor and one of the best friends, family members, and human beings ever. Julia thanks Diana for her ongoing support, rare insights, and capacity to walk her talk and love with all her heart. Thanks to Henry Loomans for being a loving and caring father throughout the years and for never giving up his dreams! Thanks to Jim and Marie Fitzpatrick, loving parents and wonderful grandparents, for their ongoing love, laughter, and support. A big thanks to Anthony Godoy for his abiding love, compassion, and understanding. Thanks to Tristan Alexander, our precious new family member, who inspired us as we wrote this book and communicated in "kick code" while still in the womb. Many thanks and big hugs to all the wonderful friends, colleagues, and clients who shared their enthusiasm, stories, and life experiences — our lives are infinitely more meaningful and rich because of you! Deepest gratitude for all the mentors, teachers, visionaries, and leaders, past and present, who have positively influenced us. Everything in these pages exists because of your transforming presence. Thank you. We honor you, and we love you all.

INDEX

Index

Index

ABOUT THE AUTHORS

DIANA LOOMANS is a national speaker, bestselling author, success coach, and founder of the Quantum Success Institute. Her current books include *100 Ways to Build Esteem and Teach Values*, *The Laughing Classroom: Everyone's Guide to Teaching with Humor & Play*, *Today I Am Lovable: 365 Positive Activities for Preteens*, *Positively Mother Goose*, and the renowned children's title *The Lovable in the Kingdom of Self-Esteem*. Her popular prose can be found on greeting cards, posters, and novelty items, and her short stories appear in the *Chicken Soup for the Soul* series. She addresses business groups, educators, parents, and the public on motivational and human potential topics. Diana, who lives in Los Angeles, has been a frequent guest on radio and television. She can be reached at www.DianaLoomans.com or at DianaLoomans@aol.com.

JULIA GODOY is an author, poet, actor, and artist. She coauthored *100 Ways to Build Esteem and Teach Values* and *Positively Mother Goose* with her mother, Diana Loomans. Her short stories and poetry appear in a number of publications, including *Chicken Soup for the Soul* and *Hot Chocolate for the Soul.* She has been a guest on numerous radio and television shows and lives in Los Angeles with her husband, Anthony, and son, Tristan. She can be reached at JuliaGodoy3@aol.com.